Sammy Morris

Sammy Morris

by

Fern Neal Stocker

A Guessing Book

MOODY PRESS
CHICAGO

All Scripture quotations are from the King James Version.

Illustrations are by Virginia Hughins.

Library of Congress Cataloging in Publication Data

Stocker, Fern Neal, 1917-
    Sammy Morris.

    (A Guessing book)
    1. Morris, Samuel, 1873-1893—Juvenile literature.
2. Converts—Liberia—Biography—Juvenile literature.
I. Title.   II. Series: Stocker, Fern Neal, 1917-
Guessing book.
BV4935.M63S76   1986   280'.4 [B]   86-21794
ISBN 0-8024-5443-7 (pbk.)

2 3 4 5 6 7 Printing/LC/Year 91 90 89 88

To Barbara Allen

Contents

To You, the Reader

To You, the Reader:

A Guessing Book is the story of a famous person. As you read along in this Guessing Book, you'll come to questions you can answer by yourself.

One, two, or three guesses are given, and you can choose one, two, or three answers. Sometimes all are correct, sometimes none. (You'll find the answer as you keep reading.) Pretty soon you'll know the person in the story so well you can get the answer right every time.

It may be fun to keep track of how many guesses you get right. But if you miss one, don't worry—this isn't a test.

Read this Guessing Book and learn about Sammy Morris, a boy who believed in the power of God.

1

The Living Dead

Startled, Margol snapped, "Why you scare me?"

"You, Margol! You scare that easy? I only want to know what you are doing."

Margol met Prince Kaboo's questioning eyes. Looking ashamed, he answered, "I'm making an altar."

"Haw-wu! What for?" Prince Kaboo watched as Margol whittled.

"I'll pray and leave food for the living dead. I want them to help me." Margol pointed to himself. "The Grebos might come back."

His warning reminded them both of the

GUESS	1. river. 2. flames. 3. killings.

They remembered the killings, the flames from the burnings, and the fierce Grebo warriors.

"You, Margol! You think an altar will keep the Grebos away?" Prince Kaboo said as Margol finished his altar.

"It can't hurt," Margol called, while he searched for a three-forked branch to hold his bowl. Once he had secured it, the boys gazed upward.

"It will hold my bowl secure," Margol predicted.

"Not empty, I hope."

"No. I have told you before that I shall keep the bowl filled with food for the living dead," Margol said.

"Haw-wu! Such boasts you make. You will forget. You will eat all your food yourself."

"Ho, silly boy. Do you not remember my grandmother died last moon? She watches me every minute. I will not forget her. She will eat the food."

Margol believed his grandmother

GUESS

1. was not yet a spirit.
2. lived though she was invisible.
3. was dead but was still part of the family.

Margol believed his grandmother was one of the many living dead, who were invisible but watched his doings.

Prince Kaboo was silent for some time, then he decided

GUESS

1. to make fun of the altar.
2. to make an altar, too.
3. to dance before the altar.

Kaboo decided to make an altar, too. After discarding several wood blocks, Kaboo selected one and began carving.

"Ah! You make it too big."

"The better to feed more of the living dead. We will need great protection if the Grebos come back. I heard my father say they will."

"It must be nice to be the chief's son," Margol declared, "and hear all the important palaver."

"Father seldom lets me listen."

Prince Kaboo continued digging the wood from the center of his bowl as Margol ran off to find

1. kola beans for his bowl.

12

| GUESS |
2. seeds.
3. milk.

Margol filled his altar bowl with kola beans, seeds, a lizard, and three snails.

Satisfied, he returned to Prince Kaboo in a shady corner of the Kru village under the mango tree. Harvest time had come. The grove vibrated with sound and movement. The Kru tribe was in

| GUESS |
1. India.
2. West Africa.
3. China.

The Kru lived in Liberia, West Africa.

"I see you will never finish. Let me help," Margol offered.

"Help indeed! With luck I will finish before the sun dips low."

"Luck, you say. You'd better move your hands like the bird's wings," Margol taunted.

"You watch. When the sun dips low, my altar will be finished."

"I'll get the food. It will take many snails to fill that big bowl." Margol slipped away into the jungle.

Prince Kaboo and Margol were

| GUESS |
1. like two beans in a kola pod.
2. enemies.
3. friends.

Margol and the prince were like two beans in a kola pod.

When Margol finally returned, the sun was setting, and the prince had

| GUESS |
1. not finished his bowl.
2. finished carving.
3. placed the bowl in a tree.

13

Prince Kaboo climbed a tall tree.

The prince had placed the bowl in a mango tree near Margol's altar.

"Ho!" Margol admitted. "Truly you did not boast!"

"Truly, it was a promise hard to keep. My hands ache."

Margol put the food safely inside the bowl. "Ah! Now the living dead will watch for us."

Prince Kaboo thought,

GUESS

1. *They can't hurt anything.*
2. *They will keep us safe.*
3. *They probably won't help.*

The prince wanted to believe the living dead would keep them safe. However, he remembered the last raid by the Grebo tribe. Now that there were so few warriors left, Kaboo wondered what would happen when the Kru's village was attacked again.

He soon learned. As the eye of the day peeped over the edge of the earth, he heard the cry "Grebos!"

Screams filled the air as fire sticks fell on the round straw huts. Prince Kaboo knew what to do. He

GUESS

1. ran.
2. fought.
3. hid.

The prince had been taught to run. Amidst the clattering and clanging of flashing spears, he wasted no time splashing with the other children across the river and climbing a tall tree.

From his precarious perch, he watched the women help little children across the murky river. The Grebos circled the village, throwing fire sticks. Prince Kaboo snorted. "Worthless goats! Worthless goats!" He saw the Kru as they shot arrows, shouted orders, and beat the flames until the fire finally forced them outside the village, where warriors were killed or captured.

Prince Kaboo

1. screamed for them to stop.

15

GUESS

2. trembled with rage.
3. threw stones across the river.

The prince trembled with rage. Helpless, he clung to his branch while he watched

GUESS

1. the warriors running away.
2. Grebos stealing the cattle.
3. every hut being looted.

Prince Kaboo watched the cattle stampede, the huts being looted, and the rice being carried away.

As the Kru warriors wailed, he covered his face. "Oh, look at the blood!" he moaned. "If only I could do something."

When the Grebo tribe took their captives and plunder away, Prince Kaboo shinnied down the tree and hurried across the river. He stamped out the sputtering fire left in the village. He gawked at the heap of cinders that had been the chief's hut. Swaying and shuffling, he wandered over the well-trodden ground, calling, "Father! Mother!"

His eyes fell on the mango tree where he had placed his bowl. The branches were burned, and the altar was black, but the charred food remained.

Kaboo stared at his altar for a long time. "So," he said. "So this is how you protect me."

The prince huddled against the tree, with his head down and his shoulders hunched. There the chief found him. "Come now, Son. Your mother will worry," he said gently. "Your sister is safe, but Margol is dead."

The prince wailed. Suddenly, he turned and looked back at Margol's altar. "He thought you would protect him!" he said to the living dead.

2

The Voice

The Kru crept back to their charred village. They didn't know the year was 1885; they only knew that today was a day never to be forgotten.

Chief Kaboo hugged his little prince tightly. "Where is Mother?" they asked each other.

Mother was

GUESS

1. killed.
2. captured.
3. safe.

Mother joined the wretched group last. She had remained on the other side of the river until every little child was safely across. Along with Kaboo's little sister, Yout, the four of them cleaned up the burned straw and struggled to build another hut.

Almost everyone had lost a family member. With heavy hearts they scratched through the ruins seeking food.

One thing was plentiful:

1. garden vegetables.

| GUESS |
2. cattle.

3. palm branches.

The Grebos had ruined their gardens and stolen most of their animals and rice, but they had plenty of palms to build huts.

The Kru stayed alive by

| GUESS |
1. eating roots, raw monkeys, and coconuts.

2. going to the market.

3. eating food sent from America.

Roots, raw monkeys, and coconuts were their main food until they could harvest new gardens and start new herds.

As Prince Kaboo grew older, the village grew stronger. And as the children grew, they were filled with a hatred for the Grebos.

One way to get revenge was

| GUESS |
1. to chant against the Grebos.

2. to bomb them.

3. to shoot them.

Prince Kaboo and the other youths spent long hours dancing and chanting against the Grebos. Word spread that the young men Kru were planning revenge. Though they were children during the last raid, they now considered themselves the warriors of the tribe.

About that time the Grebos decided to

| GUESS |
1. attack the village again.

2. forget about the Kru.

3. get other tribes to help them.

The Grebos told other villages that Chief Kaboo was planning to conquer all the people along the coast. The tribes banded together to attack the poor Kru.

Again, they attacked at

18

GUESS

1. noon.
2. sunrise.
3. twilight.

At sunrise, while the Kru were still asleep, the second slaughter took place. This time Prince Kaboo

GUESS

1. ran away.
2. stayed to fight.
3. hid in the bushes.

Prince Kaboo stayed to fight but was captured immediately. He felt a blow to his head, and stars showered around him. When he awoke, his hands were tied and his ankles chained. He realized he was in the land of the Grebos, separated from everything he knew.

His captors demanded that the Kru give them

GUESS

1. ivory.
2. palm nuts.
3. India rubber.

All three products were demanded monthly. As each full moon appeared in the sky, the Kru brought ivory, nuts, and rubber, but the Grebos always said it was not enough for the life of the prince. Chief Kaboo offered all his possessions and even his daughter, Yout.

"No, Father, I can bear the beatings better than my sister," the prince objected. "Let me remain."

Prince Kaboo was

GUESS

1. forced to work from sunrise to sunset.
2. treated well.
3. whipped.

19

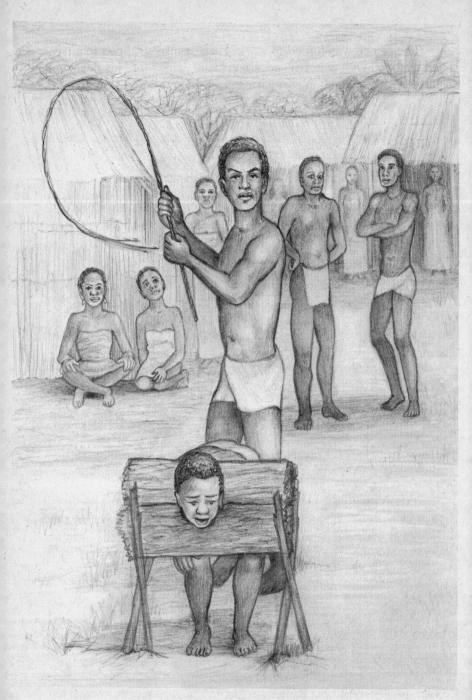

"I must escape."

The prince was forced to work. He was also strapped to a tree and whipped with a thorny, poisonous vine, which tore his flesh and started a fiery infection. Prince Kaboo's body burned. He grew

GUESS

1. sad.
2. weak.
3. angry.

As Kaboo grew weaker, he became angry and desperate. *I must do something,* he thought. He decided to

GUESS

1. cry.
2. try to escape.
3. beg for mercy.

His only hope was to escape.

One day his masters beat him in the sight of all the camp and placed his neck in a stock. The stock was

GUESS

1. two wooden beams that close over the neck.
2. valuable papers.
3. iron chains.

Two wooden beams clamped over his neck. His head protruded from the hole. Then the Grebos left him alone to suffer. He saw the blood oozing from his wounds, and fear gripped him. "I must escape, or I die," he gasped. He

GUESS

1. strained to push the two beams apart.
2. called for help.
3. clapped his hands.

Kaboo strained to push the beams apart. To his surprise, one beam moved. With his hands, he forced the loose beam away from his neck.

Someone had

	1. forgotten to lock the beams.
GUESS	2. felt sorry for him and unlocked the beam.
	3. sent a spirit to rescue him.

Kaboo never knew why the beam was loose, but he didn't waste time wondering. He

	1. sang a song.
GUESS	2. said a prayer.
	3. ran away.

Kaboo ran as fast as he could. He thought he heard a voice ordering him, "Flee, flee!"

Swiftly, he fled to the forest. *Do not take the path,* he told himself and stumbled into the bush. He squirmed between roots and scratched his way through the tall brush.

Poisonous cobras, lizards, and vipers lay in wait, but Kaboo didn't fear them as much as he feared

	1. the cannibals.
GUESS	2. the natives.
	3. the Grebos.

Fear of being returned to the Grebos haunted him most. Even the great python and the glaring eyes of the leopards seemed less than the anger of the Grebos. Exhausted, Prince Kaboo finally slept in a hollow tree. Tomorrow he would face the jungle again.

3

Discovery

As the eye of the day fanned its light through the jungle branches, Kaboo stirred and opened his eyes. For a moment he lay motionless, forgetting the horrors that had brought him to the hollow tree. Then the events crowded back: the whippings, the stock, the voice saying, "Flee, flee!" and his mad dash away.

He struggled to sit, then fell back. With another great effort, he pulled himself upright. He was giddy with thirst, and his limbs felt stiff and sore. He heard

GUESS

1. rippling water.
2. slithering snakes.
3. twittering birds.

The sound of running water roused him. He jumped to the ground, plunged his face into a pool, and drank deeply. He let the water slowly run down his swollen throat. It brought new life to Kaboo. He sighed. "I must find food." But for the moment he lay there, content to know he was safe from the Grebos.

The Grebos! Was he really safe yet? Would a warrior find him in that quiet space? *I must hurry as far away as possible. I must keep close watch for warriors.*

Kaboo was awake, now—alert. He plucked a lime from a near-by tree and rubbed it into his wounds. Soon the swelling would be gone.

Not knowing which way to go he decided

GUESS
1. to climb to higher ground.
2. to follow the stream.
3. to follow a faint animal trail.

Kaboo decided to follow the stream. It was easier to jump from rock to rock than to fight the fierce bush, which scratched and tore his flesh. As he passed overhanging berry bushes, he grasped a handful of berries. Once he lifted a rock and gathered a handful of

GUESS
1. dirt.
2. grubs.
3. roots.

Kaboo gathered grubs to eat. He liked them better fried on hot stones, but he was in a hurry.

At first he often stopped to listen for approaching warriors. As the day wore on, he grew more reckless. "I don't know where I'm going, but I'm glad for the good space between me and the Grebos." He began to feel

GUESS
1. afraid.
2. safer.
3. dreamy.

Kaboo walked rapidly. Leaping from one flat stone to another was easy for him, and somehow he felt pulled onward. Each step brought feelings of freedom and safety.

He was almost around a turn when he heard voices. Quickly he

1. rushed ahead.

| GUESS |
2. hid in the bushes.
3. swam underwater.

Kaboo hid in the bushes beside the shallow stream and saw men watering their oxen. Breathlessly, he waited. *They are not Grebos, but they might take me back for a reward. I must be careful,* Kaboo reminded himself.

When the men were gone, Kaboo hurried past the watering hole. He watched carefully as the alligators slithered back to their favorite rocks.

Kaboo realized the stream was getting deeper, the rocks fewer, and the alligators more numerous. Here the banks were sandy, however, and he raced across the sand until he came to an overgrowth that forced him back into the stream. Sometimes he had to swim around the jungle growth, but he preferred to jump from rock to rock. He continued to spend his nights in trees and to follow the stream by day.

The stream widened into a river, and Kaboo kept following it. As the water increased, Kaboo encountered more and more people. At first, he hid, but after a few weeks he felt safe enough to hurry by without speaking. No one seemed to notice him.

He took time to eat

| GUESS |
1. mangoes.
2. wild bananas.
3. ham and eggs.

Breakfast was usually bananas and mangoes.

Vines trailed like aerial ropes from high branches, and the jungle foliage was so thick that it shut out the sunlight. Ferns grew higher than a tall man's head; blossoms floated on the river. Kaboo caught his breath at the beauty.

The river gradually slowed its rush and widened.

One day as Kaboo looked off to the southeast, his heart gave a jump, and he strained forward. He saw

1. a white house.

GUESS
2. a southern mansion.
3. a native hut.

Never before had he seen a large wooden house painted white. Never before had he seen round pillars reaching as high as a tree. Never before had he seen a slate roof, a white fence, or dozens of glass windows. Once his eyes recovered from that sight, he noticed hillsides covered with rows of bushes, and men, women, and children picking berries. How strange the people looked covered with cloth.

Kaboo crept closer. He circled the strange fields. "The people are picking little dark brown fruits, a kind I never saw before. No one eats them, so why do they pick them and drop them in their heavy baskets?" They were picking

GUESS
1. coffee beans.
2. bananas.
3. berries.

Before he knew it, Kaboo was at the far end of the field, and coming toward him was a boy about his size, who was dragging a basket. As Kaboo was about to turn away, he was stunned by the boy's face. He was a Kru. Kaboo stepped from the trees and walked toward the boy, who suddenly dropped his basket and ran forward. "Prince Kaboo! What are you doing here? Is it truly you?"

"Truly, Locust! It is I. But what are you doing here?"

"I'm picking coffee beans. This is a plantation of the Conges. I work here." As though reminded by his own words, he gathered his scattered beans into his basket and continued picking.

"Ho, Prince Kaboo, walk beside me so we can talk. It is so good to speak in Nigrite again."

"What else do you speak? And who are the Conges? I never heard of that tribe."

"They are not a tribe. They were stolen from different tribes in Africa. They were sent to America as slaves and now are returned to Liberia as free men. They speak English and hire many tribespeople who speak various tribal languages. So in order to talk to each other, we all learned English. But what of you? Tell me about yourself."

Kaboo related his adventures, concluding with, "Now I'm far from the Grebos. But I don't know what to do."

Locust suggested that Kaboo

| GUESS |

1. go to sea.
2. work on the plantation.
3. put on some clothes.

Locust said, "Why don't you ask for work here on the plantation? I'll take you to Mr. Davis, the owner."

"Are you sure he won't send me back to the Grebos?" Kaboo asked.

"No, not he. He was a slave himself—remember I told you!" Just then

| GUESS |

1. a whistle blew.
2. the sun went down.
3. a bell sounded.

When the bell sounded, the workers put their baskets on their heads and walked to the weighing place. Kaboo stood aside watching the tired faces and hearing the strange words. Finally everyone was gone but Locust, Kaboo, and Mr. Davis.

Locust approached Mr. Davis. Pointing at Kaboo, he explained his situation. Mr. Davis looked sharply at Kaboo, who appeared forlorn and lonely. Walking to the prince, he took both his hands and spoke words that Kaboo could not understand.

However, he understood the smile, the warm, firm hands, and the welcoming look in Mr. Davis's eyes.

"He's asking you if you want to work on the plantation," Locust explained.

"Truly, truly." Kaboo's eyes widened, and his teeth shone white as the clouds. "Tell him 'a bird in the hand is worth a hundred flying.' I will gladly do this, for now."

Mr. Davis patted him on the head, motioned to Locust, and pointed to a frame bunkhouse.

Locust took Kaboo by the hand. "Come on. Let me show you around. The bunkhouse has boards built all around the walls; it has six places for beds in the middle. Everyone has his own mat and a change of clothes. You take a bath every night, put on the clean clothes, and are set for the next day."

"You work every day?"

"No, on Saturday we can go to town, and Sunday we go to church. And speaking of church, I am no longer *Locust*. I am *Nathan Strong*. When you become a Christian, you get a new Christian name."

"What is a Christian?" Kaboo asked.

"You will find out, Prince Kaboo. It will be the happiest day of your life. Wait and see!" Nathan promised as he led his friend to the dining room.

The two young friends ate at a table where the workers chattered in English. Kaboo nodded to the others, but he didn't say anything. He was still stunned at the turn his life had taken.

4

With Heads Held High

To Kaboo, life on the plantation was

GUESS

1. fun.
2. strange.
3. difficult.

In the Kru village, Kaboo had been looked upon as a future chief. Even the Grebos knew he was a prince and beat him more because of it. On the plantation he was just another worker. It was strange. The boss showed him how to

GUESS

1. pick brown coffee beans quickly.
2. leave the green beans undisturbed.
3. pull the basket along the row.

All of those were his duties, and steady diligence was expected.
Nathan paired up with him. They faced each other on opposite sides of one row. Kaboo despaired as he viewed the long, long row.
"Don't think of the end, just pick," Nathan advised.

The noisy chatter of other boys filled the air. "What are they saying?" Kaboo asked.

Nathan interpreted the chatter.

"You watch," Beji said. "You said I was filling my basket too slow. Mine will be filled long before yours!"

"Oh, it will, will it? We shall see!" Tunji replied.

"Yes, we shall! We shall indeed. I shall fill two baskets before you fill one!"

Kaboo watched their arms reaching out, feeling about, grasping a bean, picking it, dropping it into the basket, and reaching out again.

Someone began chanting rhythmic sayings. Much later, Beji said,

GUESS

1. "Slow as a worm, you are."
2. "I told you I'd finish first."
3. "I shall finish first next time. I shall."

Beji finished first and enjoyed calling his friend a slow worm. Immediately they began another contest. Kaboo was caught up in the cheerful rhythm and found

GUESS

1. he worked slower.
2. he worked faster.
3. he chanted instead of working.

Even the prince worked faster, but he felt insulted when Nathan finished his side and came halfway back on Kaboo's side before he could finish.

"Never mind, friend," Nathan said. "I was slow when I started."

"One day I'll finish first!" Kaboo promised. "See if I don't."

"You know, 'It is one thing to cackle and another to lay an egg.' " Nathan laughed.

Kaboo improved. The eye of the day shown hot, and Kaboo was thankful when everyone stopped a few minutes for water. He noticed Beji and Tunji were the first to go back to pick. He wondered if

GUESS

1. he could be their friend.
2. he could chatter in English.
3. he could work as fast as they did.

The English chatter of Beji and Tunji amazed Kaboo. He wished he could speak English.

When Kaboo weighed his beans at the end of the day, every part of his body ached. "It is worse than a whipping."

"You get used to it—honest!" Nathan vowed.

Mr. Davis suggested Kaboo spend an hour every day

GUESS

1. studying Greek.
2. studying English.
3. studying a native language.

Mr. Davis's wife taught the boys for an hour a day in English.

Kaboo told Nathan, "I see you never belong here if you can't speak or understand English."

Mrs. Davis loved teaching but didn't speak a word of Nigrite. She did not let that stop her, however. She had taught natives from many tribes before.

All day Kaboo listened for words he had learned in class. He also asked Nathan about other words. English was like a great puzzle to be solved.

When Sunday came, Nathan urged him, "Come to church. The missionaries usually speak in English first. Then the elder repeats what was said. As you learn more English, you find yourself understanding even before the elder speaks." Nathan twisted a cloth as he spoke.

Kaboo laughed. "Twisting that cloth won't make me go to church. I want to go to church because

1. I want to learn English."

GUESS 2. I want to know about Christians."

3. I want to see the world."

Kaboo said, "You said I'd learn about Christians. Now I *am* curious about the change in you—about your new name. I'll go."

Though many people were waiting when the wagons rolled up, Kaboo noticed many missing workers.

"Where are the others?" he asked.

"Some go into town and stay Saturday night. Some sleep. You see, Mr. Davis sends the wagons, but we don't go unless we want to," Nathan explained.

On the way to the church, Kaboo admired the green hills sloping down to the lazy river. Many hills were covered with coffee bean bushes. As they passed other plantation homes, Kaboo said, "Tell me more about the Conges. Mr. Davis looks like us, but he is—"

"I know what you mean," Nathan broke in. "They say the former slaves from America are

GUESS 1. Christians."

2. civilized."

3. the elite."

"They call them civilized and the elite. I guess that means they don't kill, eat, or make slaves of other people," Nathan finished lamely.

Kaboo's next question was cut short when the band of people in the creaking wagons began to sing Christian songs in English. Kaboo was transported with joy. The only music he had ever heard was the beating of drums or chants. "This music flows like the water," he told Nathan.

When they saw the church in the distance, Kaboo asked "Why does it have a high peak?"

Nathan answered,

GUESS 1. "That proves it's a church."

2. "It points to heaven."

32

3. "It has a finger."

Nathan thought the steeple pointed to heaven. Before Kaboo could ask, "What's heaven?" the workers jumped from the wagon, and Kaboo started to run toward the white church.
Nathan called,

| GUESS |

1. "Wait."
2. "We walk slowly to the church."
3. "Not so fast."

Nathan explained, "See how the others go with their heads high. We walk slowly to the church."
"Why?" demanded Kaboo.
"Well, I don't know. It's civilized or Christian or something. But nobody talks or asks questions when the missionary speaks."
"I'll do what you do, Nathan." Suddenly Kaboo began to question his actions. As a prince he had moved or spoken when he wanted to. Suddenly he wondered if his behavior was correct.
He followed Nathan to the back of the room where all the plantation workers sat. After they were settled, family after family of the Conges entered. Holding their heads high, they took their places near the front of the church. Everyone stared at

| GUESS |

1. the men's frock coats and stove pipe hats.
2. the women's gathered skirts, braided bodices, and large hats.
3. the children's frocks, hose, and shoes.

Kaboo opened his mouth, but Nathan quickly put his finger over it. *Questions will have to wait,* he seemed to say.
Since Kaboo was gawking at the Conges, he did not notice the missionaries and elders enter and take their places.
Suddenly organ music filled the church. Kaboo could not believe so many tones could come from a small box. His eyes popped open, and Nathan covered his lips once more.
The Conges opened books and upon a signal began singing

Family after family entered.

with the organ. Most of the plantation workers knew the songs and sang the words whether they understood or not. Evidently there were not enough books for all.

Kaboo listened in awe to the music. His soul felt soothed. The talking, however, excited him. The missionaries' words in English were not understandable, and the interpretation was in another native language. But he did understand

GUESS	1. the earnest expressions on their faces.
	2. the reverence with which they touched the Bible.
	3. the happiness in their voices.

Prince Kaboo sat spellbound. "I must learn about this God."

5

Two Cows' Tails

Every day Mrs. Davis began the English class the same way. "How many ears have you?"

The class answered in unison, "We have two ears!"

"Then add a third, and listen to what I have to tell you!"

She never explained what she meant, but Kaboo listened. First, he understood "ears," then "two ears," then "listen." Finally the meaning filled his head. He grinned and nodded. "Yes, Mrs. Davis, I will listen with three ears, here and everywhere!" He said this under his breath. He had learned, at last, not to speak out.

Kaboo learned English

> GUESS

1. in the fields.
2. in the bunkhouse.
3. at the table.

Not only did Kaboo learn English in the classroom but everywhere. When he went to town with Nathan, he discovered more new words. Learning and understanding was one thing—writing and speaking another.

As he entered the bunkhouse one day, he saw Nathan on his knees, both hands lifted up and his face upturned. "What are you doing?" Kaboo asked.

"I am talking to God."

"Who is your God; the God of the Kru people or the God in the church?"

Nathan answered, "In a way they are the same, the Creator. Remember we learned God created man so that the sun would have someone for whom to shine. Then God created plants and animals for food for man; then a wife to talk to."

"Do the missionaries teach the same?" Kaboo asked doubtfully.

"Almost the same," Nathan nodded.

"What is different?" Kaboo wanted to know.

Nathan took a deep breath, "Well, you know how we had a god of war, a god of sickness, a god of the lake, a god of cattle, and all those other gods?"

"Yes."

"The Christians say

GUESS

1. there are three gods."
2. there is one God."
3. there are many gods."

"The missionaries say there is only one God. He is all powerful, all strong, all knowing," Nathan explained.

"And what of the spirits and the living dead?"

"The Christians believe in one Spirit, the Holy Spirit."

"And the living dead?"

"When a person dies, Christians believe his soul goes to heaven if he was a believer—and to hell if he was not."

"Then he doesn't stay and watch his people? There is no need to make altars and leave food for the living dead?"

"No, not at all."

Kaboo's eyes filled with tears. "I found that out the night of the Grebo's attack, but I thought I was the only one who knew. Poor Margol!"

The two friends talked a long time. Kaboo finally asked, "And who is your God, Nathan?"

"He is my Father."

"Then you hold up your hands, kneel, and talk to your Father. Do it now." Kaboo knelt with Nathan.

He knelt again the next Sunday in the churchyard. A new missionary had arrived, Miss Knolls of Fort Wayne, Indiana. She was telling the story of Saul of Tarsus after the church service. Nathan repeated her words to Prince Kaboo. When she spoke of Saul's hearing the voice from heaven, Kaboo burst out, "That's just what I heard—a voice telling me what to do! It said to flee, flee!"

After Miss Knolls finished her story, she turned to Kaboo. With Nathan translating, they talked long and seriously. Kaboo believed

GUESS	1. the Holy Spirit called.
	2. God directed him.
	3. Jesus was his Savior.

Kaboo believed God had directed him to this mission. And after many weeks of instruction he believed that Jesus was his Savior.

Miss Knolls spent many hours every Sunday teaching Kaboo. He was her first convert, and a strong bond of friendship linked the two.

To celebrate Kaboo's conversion, Miss Knolls gave him a new name.

She said, "When I went to a school named Taylor University, a banker helped me. I shall give you his name. From now on you shall be known as *Samuel Morris*."

Kaboo was happy. "Like Saul, I got a new name! And like the boy Samuel of the Bible, God spoke to me. How lucky I am!"

"Lucky? Not lucky, Kaboo—I mean Sammy. Can't you see God has chosen you?" Miss Knolls smiled.

Nathan and Sammy continued their work and studies at the coffee plantation until the picking season was over. Sammy was surprised

GUESS	1. at the sum of money he received.
	2. when his job ended.
	3. at something Miss Knoll suggested.

Miss Knolls suggested that Sammy move to Monrovia, where

39

the mission had its headquarters. She cautioned him to spend his money wisely and introduced him to a house painter.

"Come be my helper," said the painter. The Conges have built a great college here, and I am commissioned to paint it. You can sleep on a mat in the rooms we are painting and take your meals with the missionaries."

"And what of Nathan?"

"Nathan can come too. I have also engaged a third boy. You three will have much work to do."

Sammy and Nathan decided

GUESS

1. to paint.
2. to run away.
3. to go back to their tribe.

Sammy and Nathan went to Monrovia, the capital of Liberia. And in spite of Miss Knoll's warning, Sammy soon spent his money. He bought clothes, a mat, and a pair of strange scissors. He cut his own hair and Nathan's. His system was simple. He cut off almost all his hair. Soon he had a curly cap that was quite comfortable.

"Alabo, let me cut your hair, too," Sammy suggested as the boys lay on their mats after working all day.

"How did you learn to cut hair?" Alabo queried.

"Look this way. See how I cut mine. Look at Nathan; I cut his hair too," Sammy coaxed.

"Oh, all right," Alabo yielded, "but be careful with those points. I don't wish to lose an eye."

Sammy

GUESS

1. liked life in the city.
2. hated the city.
3. hated his new friend.

Sammy enjoyed his new work, his new friends, and the close contact with the missionaries.

When they ran out of paint, Sammy would

GUESS

1. hunt up the missionaries.
2. roam the city.
3. play on the beach.

Sammy hunted for the missionaries. There were several near Monrovia besides Miss Knolls. Reverend C. E. Smirl and Miss Munsee spent hours answering questions. For two years Sammy learned everything he could.

He passed on his knowledge to Nathan and took Alabo by the hand. He took Alabo to

GUESS

1. the church.
2. the missionaries.
3. the school.

First, he took Alabo to church and introduced him to the missionaries. Then he talked to him of God.

"What does your tribe say of the first man and woman?"

Alabo found that question easy. "Ho, we learn they had everything they wanted in paradise."

"What happened?"

"God told them not to eat the eggs of the birds," Nathan responded.

"Did they eat them?" Sammy questioned further.

"Yes, they ate, and God separated from them."

"Was there a way to get back to God?" Sammy persisted.

"No, no way."

"That is how Christianity is different. The Bible shows a way to get to God. He sent His Son to take the punishment of man. Jesus Christ made a way by dying in place of all men—for all sin."

Alabo was silent for a time. "What do I have to do to get to God?" he finally asked.

"Believe on the Lord Jesus Christ, and thou shalt be saved." Sammy was glad he had memorized the verse from the Bible and could recite it to Alabo.

"That's all you have to do—just believe?"

"That's all He asks!" Sammy paused, then knelt, raised his hands to heaven, and prayed.

41

Alabo soon followed. "O, God, I believe in your Son. Save my soul."

The missionaries baptized both young men, using their new names, Sammy Morris and Henry O'Neil.

Every spare minute Sammy and Henry

GUESS	1. worked overtime.
	2. helped the missionaries.
	3. played.

They helped the missionaries as much as they could.

Fearful and trembling, Sammy gave his first testimony. Miss Knolls helped him with the English words. "Ask the Holy Spirit to help you to be brave," she suggested.

Once Sammy started speaking, fear left him, and he was able to say, "God spoke to me. He said, 'Flee, Flee'; so I ran away from the Grebos. God directed me to the plantation. I could have been eaten by cannibals or harmed by wild beasts, but God protected me. He led Miss Knolls around the world to tell me about Jesus, my Savior. I thank Him." Sammy sat down, exhausted.

Sammy and Henry helped the missionaries by

GUESS	1. singing religious songs.
	2. praying at meetings.
	3. ringing bells.

Sammy and Henry sang in church, in street meetings, and at prayer meetings. They gave their testimonies and prayed.

When three Monrovian women started prayer meetings lasting from midnight to daylight, Sammy and Henry joined them. They prayed for hours. In time

GUESS	1. no one else came.
	2. a few old women came.
	3. fifty young people accepted Christ.

42

When fifty young people were saved, the three women rejoiced and praised the Lord for sending Sammy and Henry.

Sammy grew more convinced that he should be a missionary to his own tribe.

"Reverend Smirl, what must I do to be a missionary?" Sammy asked.

"You cannot just go back to your tribe, even if it were safe. You are not ready. You are lacking in education." Mr. Smirl held up a heavy book.

"How can I get an education?" Sammy persisted.

"You can go to America. It only costs a hundred dollars for a fare across the ocean," Mr. Smirl encouraged. "Save your money. Work long hours like Nathan."

Sammy

GUESS

1. saved his money.
2. prayed.
3. visited another missionary.

Sammy prayed and decided to visit Miss Munsee who was at a mission several miles from Monrovia. The long walk left him with throbbing feet, but when he entered the last dusty path to the mission outpost he forgot about his feet.

"Ho, Miss Munsee!" he called.

"Who comes to my door? Oh, Sammy, welcome. I'm so glad you came—just in time for devotions." In a baggy sweater, flowing skirt, and bedroom shoes, Miss Munsee held the screen door open.

Sammy stepped inside the shack. Clutter was everywhere. Books and papers were open where Miss Munsee had stopped reading. Her broken sofa served as a bed and was covered with crumpled blankets and pillows. Those she hurriedly rolled up and hid.

Sammy liked Miss Munsee. *She cannot be bothered with the world; she is full of the Bible,* he thought.

"Come, Sammy. I'm reading the fourteenth chapter of John. Listen!" Miss Munsee read the passage in which the Savior first announced to His disciples the coming of a new and powerful helper, the Holy Spirit.

Together they explored the Scriptures. Sammy asked question after question about the Holy Spirit. Miss Munsee answered until she was finally compelled to confess,

| GUESS |

1. "I have told you everything I know."
2. "That is all I know."
3. "We have read every Scripture."

Sammy persisted, "Who told you what you know about the Holy Spirit?"

"The person who helped me most was Stephen Merritt," Miss Munsee admitted.

"And where is he?"

"In New York."

"Very well," Sammy replied, "I will go to see him."

When he arrived back in Monrovia and told Miss Knolls of his decision to go to New York, she objected.

"But Sammy, what of your job; what of helping the missionaries; what of your singing and your English lessons?"

Sammy only answered, "We have a saying, 'You cannot hold onto two cows' tails at once.' "

6

The Sea

"**O** Father, help me. Let there be a ship in harbor," Sammy prayed. He was on his way to

GUESS	1. the seashore. 2. New York. 3. the Kru tribe.

Sammy hurried to the seashore. "O, God, help me get to New York. Please help me." In time he smelled the salt water and felt the warm moist breeze touch his cheeks. "It is not much farther," he told himself. A peace came over his soul, as though God had quieted his heart with an answer.

His first glimpse of the seaport showed him a ship anchored in the bay. "Thank you, Father," he said.

He asked a passing sailor, "Where is the ship headed?" The sailor replied,

GUESS	1. "Lisbon." 2. "South Africa." 3. "New York."

The sailor replied, "New York, North America."

As Sammy drew closer, a small boat pulled off from the ship and headed for shore. All the men were gray.* That didn't bother Sammy. He knew the missionaries were also gray and very kind.

He watched as the men stepped ashore, and he noticed a man giving orders in English. *That must be the captain!* he decided.

Sammy waited until the captain was near and then cried out, "My Father told me you would take me to New York to see Stephen Merritt."

Startled, the captain asked, "And where is your father?"

Sammy replied,

GUESS

1. "In New York."
2. "In Africa."
3. "In heaven."

Sammy looked the captain in the eye and said, "In heaven."

The captain swore the first oath Sammy had heard in English. "My ship does not carry passengers. You must be crazy!" He tossed the words over his shoulder as he strode across the sand.

"The captain must come back here to get into his small boat," Sammy reasoned. "I will not move from this spot."

All day Sammy waited. He had nothing to eat but dared not leave.

Late that night the crew returned.

"Please, Mr. Captain, take me to New York! Please!" Sammy pleaded.

The captain kicked in Sammy's direction. "I'll give you a swift kick if you don't stop bothering me. I will not take you!" The captain boarded the boat and set off with several drunk sailors.

"Oh, yes, you will," Sammy shouted.

He slept on the sandy seashore. "Father, please change the captain's mind," he prayed.

Although Sammy had had nothing to eat for two days, he stayed on the spot. The next morning the captain and a few crewmen again came ashore.

*White men.

46

The Kru boy hurried up to him, saying,

<table>
<tr><td rowspan="3">GUESS</td><td>1. "Please take me."</td></tr>
<tr><td>2. "I want to go."</td></tr>
<tr><td>3. "My Father says you will take me this time."</td></tr>
</table>

Sammy said, "My Father says you will take me this time."

It so happened that two of the crew had deserted ship the previous day, leaving the captain shorthanded.

"You are a Kru, right?" the captain said, having known experienced Kru sailors in the past. "What do you want?"

"Just take me to New York to see Stephen Merritt," replied Sammy. "That's all I ask."

The captain turned to the boat crew and said, "Take him to the ship!" Little did the captain know that Sammy was not an experienced sailor.

On boarding the vessel, Sammy found a young man with a wound in his leg lying on the deck. Sammy knelt down and prayed for him and then asked for water and bandages to bind up the fellow's leg.

When the grateful youth regained his strength, he said, "I'm Harold, the cabin boy. Who are you?" He heard Sammy's story and realized the Kru had not eaten for several days.

"Leaping lizards, you must be hungry!" Harold said to Sammy as he led him to the galley.

The cook, however, refused. "I ain't got no orders to feed him," he stated. And he called Sammy a name.

Harold hid Sammy from the cook. He asked for food for himself, which he shared with Sammy.

"What did the cook mean?" Sammy asked.

Harold looked blankly at Sammy. "Oh, lots of people call others names just because of their color. I think they are fools, but there *is* one on board, a Malay. You better stay out of *his* way."

"Just because I'm black?" Sammy asked. "All my Kru people are black. The only gray people I've seen until now are the missionaries, and they were good."

Harold looked at Sammy with pity. He said,

47

	1. "The sailors are good, too."
GUESS	2. "The sailors are bad."
	3. "The sailors are as bad as the missionaries are good."

Harold told Sammy the sailors were as bad as the missionaries were good.

Later, Sammy had cause to believe him.

The captain came out to the ship late that night and questioned Sammy.

"You mean you are a complete landlubber?" He gazed at Sammy in disbelief. "You will have to be put ashore at once!"

"Why?" demanded Sammy. "I'll work as hard as any man."

"You'll be sick, that's what you'll be—sick and useless. This ship is a three-hundred-and-fifty-foot three-master. That means it rides rough."

"Oh, I won't be sick, I promise. I'll work every day," Sammy pleaded.

Harold stepped up. "Please take him, Captain. He helped me. He is strong and willing. Please."

"I must be crazy," the captain admitted looking at the pair. "I know better, but something tells me to keep him."

After that, every word that was said to Sammy was accompanied by

	1. a curse.
GUESS	2. a kick.
	3. a slap.

Everyone felt free to kick or slap Sammy. Curses and vile language rained on his head. It was just as well he didn't understand all the words.

All the crew lived in dread of the captain. It was a motley group picked up from the four quarters of the globe. Sammy was the only black and was resented at once. The crew began to plan to do away with him.

On the third night out, they lashed Sammy to a spar in the

48

ship's rigging, where he could help reef the sails and pull the ropes.
That night a tropical storm came up suddenly.

<table>
<tr><td rowspan="3">GUESS</td><td>1. It caught the ship with canvas spread.</td></tr>
<tr><td>2. There was no time to reef the sail.</td></tr>
<tr><td>3. They had to ride out the storm.</td></tr>
</table>

There was nothing to do but ride out the storm.

All around Sammy now was a world of rumbling water, gray in the hollows, greenish on the slopes. The wind tore off the foaming crests and flung spray at the ship, striking it savagely.

Sammy prayed, "Father, I am not afraid, for I know that You will take care of me. But could you make it so that I won't have to come up here?" Somehow the sound of his own voice reassured Sammy.

The day darkened, and a burst of lightning lit up the sea with supernatural brilliance. A crack of thunder shattered the world. Lightning again struck the hissing water. Sammy watched with fascinated eyes. He saw

<table>
<tr><td rowspan="3">GUESS</td><td>1. mountains of dark water.</td></tr>
<tr><td>2. the attack of wind.</td></tr>
<tr><td>3. the stinging spray.</td></tr>
</table>

The worst part was the spray that stung the boy's flesh, blinded his eyes, and chilled him to the bone.

The spar on which Sammy was tied was often under water. He swallowed so much seawater that he became deathly ill.

When the sailors at last untied him and brought him down to the foot of the mast, he fell in a heap. The captain came up and kicked him. "I knew this would happen," he growled.

Sammy got to his knees, sick as he was, and lifted his hands in prayer. "Father, You know I promised to work for this man every day till I got to America. I cannot work when I'm sick like this. Please take away this sickness."

The sailors gasped when he

| GUESS |

1. rose to his feet.
2. resumed his tasks.
3. was not ill.

He was never ill again on that ship.

Next afternoon, Harold came up to him, saying, "Sam, I heard you praying during that storm. I don't like it below decks, and you are not trained to work in the rigging. Let's trade places."

"Thank You, Lord, for answering my prayer," Sammy murmured.

"The only thing I hate is that I won't see much of you anymore," he told Harold.

"We always know we are friends." Harold clasped Sammy's hands.

Promptly Sammy reported to the captain for duty. Unfortunately, the captain had been drinking and struck Sammy with his fist when told of the trade in jobs. He knocked Sammy to the floor where he lay unconscious for several hours. When he regained consciousness, he started working around the cabin as cheerfully as if nothing had happened.

Somewhat sobered, the captain watched him. He heard Sammy

| GUESS |

1. sing about Jesus.
2. pray for him.
3. sweep the floor.

Memories of his mother flooded the mind of the captain. "She sang the same songs to me when I was a boy," the captain marveled. "She taught me, 'What is learned in the cradle lasts till the grave.' "

7

Seaworthy

Because the storm wrenched the superstructure of the ship, the captain anchored to the leeward of a small, uncharted island. While the caulkers and carpenters were busy, the rest of the crew manned the pumps.

Sammy was expected to keep up with the seasoned sailors. He pumped and prayed and prayed and pumped.

"There, have some rum. Twill warm yer insides," one of the sailors invited.

"No, no," Sam refused. "The Holy Spirit will warm me and give me strength." Sammy said it bravely, but when the pains of fatigue almost overpowered him, he had to pray again. For two weeks they pumped. Sammy was about to faint when they hoisted the anchor. He didn't know it, but the sailors

GUESS

1. plotted to get rid of him.
2. respected him now.
3. laughed at him.

Since Sammy had pumped equally with the most seasoned sailor, the rough seamen now respected him.

The captain ordered extra rations of rum to celebrate the lifting of the anchor. As the sun dipped low, a free-for-all fight broke out. Someone insulted the Malay, who seized a cutlass.

Sammy saw the Malay rushing toward some of his shipmates. The Malay's face showed the murder that was in his heart.

Sammy

| GUESS | 1. stepped between the Malay and the men.
2. ran to the captain's quarters.
3. told the Malay to behave himself. |

Sammy stepped between the Malay and the men. Quietly he said, "Don't kill. Don't kill."

"Don't kill!" laughed the Malay. "I've killed many a black, you can believe. I hate blacks, I do! Get out of my way, or I'll kill you—now!"

Sammy advanced to meet him. The Malay raised his cutlass and scowled.

Sammy

| GUESS | 1. looked him straight in the eye.
2. moved to defend himself.
3. put his hands over his face. |

Sammy looked the Malay straight in the eye for several moments. The Malay

| GUESS | 1. went back to his cabin.
2. lowered his weapon.
3. shivered. |

The Malay shivered because of God's power. He lowered his weapon and went to his cabin.

One of the crewmen whispered, "Just because the river is quiet, don't think the crocodiles have left."

The captain, hearing the noise, rushed to the deck in time to see the Malay slip away and the crew cease fighting. "What power does this boy have?" he marveled.

Together they went below deck, and Sammy dropped to his knees in the captain's quarters. "Oh, Father, thank You for overpowering the Malay. Thank You for peace on board this ship. Dear Father, forgive the captain and make him whole."

The captain, having known the gospel from his youth, now surrendered. "Oh, God, You know I've run away from You many times, but now I'm asking You to save my soul."

After prayers, Sammy and the captain

GUESS	1. sang Christian songs.
	2. talked far into the night.
	3. read the Bible.

The captain and Sammy sang and talked.

Next morning Sammy looked at the captain's quarters. Years of smoke, dirt, and filth were apparent. "The Spirit will not dwell where filth abides," he said and set to work with soap and water.

He even turned the deadly weapons hanging on the walls into decorations by polishing them.

"I'll not give you a new name," Sammy said, "but new quarters."

The captain was so pleased he invited the ship's officers to view his "new quarters." He did more:

GUESS	1. he stood while Sammy prayed.
	2. he gave the crew no rum.
	3. he invited the crew for prayer.

Since the captain invited them for prayer, several crewmen came to his quarters. There they

GUESS	1. heard Sammy's testimony.
	2. heard the captain's testimony.
	3. sang Christian songs.

53

They heard testimonies and sang songs. Mysteriously a Bible appeared on a table, and the captain read parts of the Scripture.

After the meeting, six of the group seemed reluctant to leave. "Let's go on deck for a while," the German suggested. The sailors climbed the stairs and lounged together in the fading sunset of the open sea. The men exchanged memories of home. The German told a story causing the group to laugh together. In the distance, they saw the evening star. They felt the comfortable slap, slap of the waves against the side of the ship. A pleasant warm evening surrounded them.

After a moment of silence, Sammy spoke. "Your story makes me think of a saying we have in Africa, 'Fair speech turns elephants away from the garden path.' "

The Bulgarian added, "We say, 'Gentle words open iron gates.' "

"We say, 'Ask me what is my virtue, not what is the color of my skin,' " the Arab added.

"That's nothing," the Spaniard spoke up. "In my country we say it straight out, 'White or black, we are human.' "

The German laughed. "I see you got the point of my story. In Germany we say, 'You should not hate everyone who has a different nose than you.' "

Everyone had spoken but the Slovak, who now offered, "You know I'm a loner, but this cruise has been different. I've learned the truth of a saying from my country. 'A handful of friends is better than a wagon of gold.' " A feeling of kinship grew among the crew as more sailors accepted Christ.

A few days later, the crew reported, "The Malay is dangerously ill. All hope of recovery is gone."

When Sammy heard this, he rushed to the Malay's bunk. There he stayed,

GUESS	1. spoon-feeding him.
	2. praying for him.
	3. cooling his hot forehead.

Gently Sammy bathed the big man. His prayers were answered, and the Malay recovered. Though he could speak little

English, and Sammy knew nothing of the Malayan tongue, he conveyed to Sammy that he would protect him with his very life.

"Don't give your life to me, give it to Jesus," Sammy pleaded. "God healed you, not me." The Malay did not understand, but he followed Sammy everywhere.

Several days later the captain proclaimed, "Only a few more stops and we will be ready to steer straight for New York."

The next morning the captain decided to go ashore with a stock of merchandise to barter with the natives. He

GUESS	1. took a larger crew than usual.
	2. armed his men.
	3. felt uneasy.

Because he felt uneasy, the captain instructed the lookout in the crow's nest to watch carefully and wigwag him if anything unusual happened.

When the boat was halfway to shore, the lookout shouted, "Hundreds of men are carrying light canoes!" The natives

GUESS	1. put their canoes into the water.
	2. shot out into the sea.
	3. overcame the small boat.

Led by a white man, the Africans were bent upon capturing the boat, the ship, and the cargo. They had succeeded in such an adventure a few weeks before.

Before the captain and his men could reach the ship, the small boats surrounded them. The captain ordered his men to open fire. At such close range, every shot found its mark.

As quickly as possible, the captain drew close to the ship. Now the crew on deck poured fire into the attackers. The captain and men

| GUESS | 1. climbed aboard. |
| | 2. were killed. |

3. hoisted the small boat.

The captain and his men climbed aboard on one side of the ship, but the outlaws on the other side of the ship

GUESS
1. climbed on board, too.
2. made rope ladders.
3. had a white leader.

The white leader and his followers threw rope ladders to the rail of the ship and climbed aboard.

"Surrender the ship or die!" the leader shouted.

The ship's crew had had time to climb high up in the rigging. One of these men

GUESS
1. laughed.
2. cried.
3. shot the leader.

A crewman shot the leader. A few of his followers, however, dashed for the hatch and reached the hold of the ship.

Sammy stood by the captain's side when the renegade white man was shot.

"Sam," ordered the captain, "go to my cabin, lock and bolt the door on the inside, and guard the ship's valuables. And pray, boy, pray!"

Sammy hurried to obey. The crew

GUESS
1. fastened down the hatches.
2. fought with more natives swarming aboard.
3. fell to their knees in prayer.

The crew locked the attackers inside the hold. Then they turned their attention to the swarms of natives still coming over the sides of the ship.

Sammy could see no more, but he heard

GUESS	1. the crack of guns.
	2. the thud of men falling.
	3. cries and groans of wounded.

Frightened, he heard all of that. It was a fight to death. Sammy fell on his knees and prayed, "Oh, Father, do something. Stop this horror, please, Father."

About midday a stiff breeze sprang up. The ship began to roll. No more natives could get on board. The gunfire ceased.

"Thank You, Father. Praise Your holy Name," Sammy continued to pray.

Sammy heard the click, click of the anchor chains. The ship moved. For hours he heard the tramp of heavy-booted feet on deck. Then he heard the splash of dead bodies being thrown into the sea.

At nightfall he heard

GUESS	1. the hatches opening.
	2. the crew descending.
	3. the looters overcome.

The pirates locked in the hold with the rum had drunk so much they were easily overcome.

Finally, Sammy heard a knock. "Let me in. This is the captain."

Quickly Sammy opened the door and helped the big man to his bunk. The captain seemed to faint. Sammy

GUESS	1. tore away his clothes.
	2. washed his wounds.
	3. prayed beside the bed.

When the exhausted man awoke, he found his wounds dressed and Sammy praying. Gently the captain put his arms around Sam's shoulders and drew him closer.

57

"Sammy! Your prayers have saved us and the ship. Although our men fought like demons, we were outnumbered ten to one. If the wind had not sprung up so that the ship rolled, the attackers would have swarmed over us like ants."

8

New York

> Jesus, our Shepherd, Brother, Friend,
> Our Prophet, Priest and King,
> Our Lord, our Life, our Way, our End,
> Accept the praise we bring.*

Sammy sang first; then he asked the crewmen to join with him, as the bodies of the dead sailors were reverently lowered into the sea the next day.

> Jesus, our Shepherd, Brother, Friend,
> Accept the praise we bring.

After the battle, the captain's prayer meetings packed the cabin. A pleasant atmosphere surrounded the boat, and the trip to New York was peaceful.

Sammy was busy

<table>
<tr><td rowspan="3">GUESS</td><td>1. nursing the wounded.</td></tr>
<tr><td>2. cleaning the captain's quarters.</td></tr>
<tr><td>3. helping the cook.</td></tr>
</table>

*Written by John Newton, former slave trade captain.

"What does it mean?"

Nursing and cleaning kept Sammy busy. As the voyage drew to its end, excitement mounted.

"How will you find your Stephen Merritt? Does he know you are coming? Do you have an address? Do you know how big New York is? You think you can go into the city in those rags?" The sailors questioned Sammy.

"I don't know, I don't know!" Sammy cried. "But my Father knows, and He will show me. Didn't He bring me to New York?"

The sailors had to admit defeat. "At least we can give him some clothes," the German decided.

Harold contributed a pair of cut-off green pants. The Malay wanted to give him a red greatcoat, but everyone laughed. "He can't walk in that heavy thing." Finally, a shirt with short sleeves was found, and also a light jacket. "It will have to do," the German sighed. "At least he has a decent cap and good shoes." The fact that the shoes were three sizes too large bothered no one.

All at once the captain shouted, "Oh, come, Sammy! See!" He pointed to

GUESS	1. the water.
	2. the Statue of Liberty.
	3. the ships.

"The Statue of Liberty is an emblem of hope for the poor," said the captain.

"What does it mean?" Sammy questioned as he gazed at the huge figure.

"It means you are welcome to America, Samuel Morris. See how new it looks. The Statue of Liberty has been here only a few years. Now you can do whatever you wish."

"I wish to see Stephen Merritt and learn about the Holy Spirit."

"You are at liberty to do so," the captain assured Sammy with a hug.

Many of the crew had

| GUESS | 1. lumps in their throats. |
| | 2. tears under their eyelids. |

3. candy in their pockets.

As they bade Sammy farewell, some felt like crying. The Malay followed him down the gangplank.

On a Friday in September 1891, Sammy walked along the wharf on the East River. No one paid any attention to the oddly dressed black boy. So intent on his mission was Sammy that he hardly noticed the streets or buildings. Finally, he saw a man as ill-dressed as he was. The man seemed to be going nowhere.

"Sir, where can I find Stephen Merritt?"

"It be Stephen Merritt you are wanting? As a matter of fact, I do know him," responded the stranger.

"Then, please, take me to him," Sammy begged.

"Not so fast, young man. This be Pike Street, and the mission is away over on Eighth Avenue. I'll take ye there for a dollar."

Sammy had not a penny, but he nodded.

He followed the tramp along many streets full of hurrying people. His eyes were filled with wonder at the sight of crowds and buildings. His ears rang with the sounds of

GUESS
1. carriage wheels rolling.
2. horses braying.
3. drivers calling.

There were many kinds of noises. The smells were the most overpowering. Garbage was on the streets, and the strong odor of garlic and smothering sooty air assailed his nostrils.

"The sailors said this was a wonderful place," he kept reminding himself. "Why is everyone in such a hurry?"

Finally his guide said, "See the man locking his door? That be Stephen Merritt, the man putting the key in his pocket."

Sammy ran forward, calling, "I am Samuel Morris. I have just come from Africa to talk with you about the Holy Spirit!"

Mr. Merritt smiled and said, "Do you have any letters of introduction?"

"No, I had no time to wait for such. I came as fast as I could."

"I see," Mr. Merritt said kindly. "I have an appointment just now, so I cannot talk. Will you step next door? See the mission sign? Stay there until I come back."

There was something in Sammy's eyes that interested Mr. Merritt. Sammy started for the mission when the tramp called out, "Where is my dollar? I brought you here. Give me a dollar!"

Sammy waved in the direction of Mr. Merritt. "Stephen Merritt will pay you."

Mr. Merritt smiled as he handed a dollar to the tramp and climbed into his coach. *Well, what will we do with this one?* he asked himself.

Sammy

> **GUESS**
> 1. ran after Mr. Merritt.
> 2. followed the tramp.
> 3. entered the mission.

Sammy entered the mission. Unkempt men lined the walls of the plain room. When he stood beside one, he was motioned to the end of the line. "Don't ever try to break into line," the beggar in front of him said. "These guys don't mess around. They wouldn't mind smacking you." As the line moved forward, Sammy moved, too. He soon saw that each man received a bowl of soup and a hunk of bread.

After his long walk, it felt good to take his soup to an empty chair and sit awhile.

"Soup tastes good," Sammy said to his neighbor.

"Only trouble with taking this soup," the fellow next to him grumbled, "is that they expects you to stay for the preaching."

"Are we having preaching?" Sammy looked around. The square room was plain, but he noticed

> **GUESS**
> 1. a box that made music.
> 2. a cross.
> 3. a pulpit.

Only the audience was different from the mission at home. These men looked even worse than the sailors. All eighteen men gave off strong odors

GUESS	1. from drink.
	2. from dirty clothes.
	3. from not washing.

The crowd smelled from drink and dirt, but no one seemed to mind except Sammy.

When finished, everyone took his spoon and bowl back to the kitchen where a rosy-faced woman was washing dishes. The men then sat down in rows of chairs facing the pulpit. Sammy followed.

Soon the meeting started. Sammy was delighted that they were singing hymns he knew. His voice filled the room.

The preacher stepped forward uncertainly. When he explained that he was learning to preach and this was his first audience, some of the men sneered. Sammy

GUESS	1. was sorry for him.
	2. remembered his first testimony.
	3. laughed at the preacher.

Sammy remembered his own first testimony and felt for the young man who read his sermon. Though it was several pages, it didn't take him long to read it. Because he had not used all his time, the preacher

GUESS	1. quit.
	2. asked for testimonies.
	3. read Scripture.

The preacher asked for testimonies.
The first to stand up was

GUESS	1. Sammy.
	2. an old man.
	3. a child.

Sammy walked to the pulpit as Miss Knolls had taught him. He gave his testimony in an English strange to the ears of the New Yorkers. He told of the Kru, the Grebos, the beatings, the voice telling him to "flee," the coffee plantation, the missionaries, and the five-month sea voyage to America.

Heads that had been drooping stretched forward. Every man in the audience was electrified by the working of God in Sammy's life.

When the youth said, "Let us pray," he knelt and lifted his hands. He did not begin until every man was kneeling in a circle around him. Then he prayed, begging the men to join in. Gradually some men prayed aloud. Some whispered their prayers while Sammy cried out to God.

Stephen Merritt, remembering his promise to join Sammy, walked into the room in the midst of the prayer. He

> GUESS
> 1. stood speechless.
> 2. prayed with the others.
> 3. stopped the meeting.

Mr. Merritt knelt and prayed with the men. The student preacher began a song, and all sang praises to God. The Spirit of God touched hearts.

After the meeting Mr. Merritt said to Sammy, "Come home with me." They left the student preacher surrounded by inquirers. Outside the mission, Sammy marveled that they were to ride in such a fine coach.

"What beautiful horses!" Sammy exclaimed. It seemed strange to be

> GUESS
> 1. stepping into a fine coach.
> 2. talking with an important preacher.
> 3. seeing the lights of New York at night.

"What makes the lights shine on the streets?" Sammy asked.

"They are gas lights," Stephen Merritt answered.

"Gas? That is a new word to me. At home we only have one eye of the night," Sammy explained.

"Never mind. We must get you to bed. It's very late."

When they arrived at the Merritt home, Sammy wanted to stay in the carriage house with the horses. "I can sleep in the hay," he pointed out.

"Oh, no. You are sleeping in the bishop's bed tonight," Mr. Merritt insisted as he led Sammy to the kitchen door of his fine home. "You brought the Spirit of God to those men tonight!"

Mrs. Merritt had

GUESS

1. waited up for her husband.
2. cooked dinner.
3. cried herself to sleep.

She had waited up. "Why, what have you here, Stephen?" she asked in surprise when she saw Sammy.

Merritt answered, "Oh, Dolly, this is an angel in ebony!"

"What are you going to do with him?" she asked.

"I am going to put him in the bishop's bed."

"Oh, no! Don't do that!" Dolly objected.

Sammy slept

GUESS

1. in the carriage house.
2. in the bishop's bed.
3. in the woodshed.

Sammy slept between sheets on the bishop's soft bed. Mr. Merritt had to show him how to use the bathroom and shower. He also drowned Sammy in the bishop's night shirt.

"When are you going to tell me about the Holy Spirit?" Sammy asked.

"Not tonight, son. It's one o'clock in the morning. Sleep well."

As the preacher started for the door, Sammy fell on his knees before the bed. Pushing up the long sleeves of the night shirt, he clasped his hands and gave thanks to his Father in heaven.

9

The Holy Spirit

"What in the world are you doing here?" Mr. Merritt chided Sammy. "I went to your room and found you gone. I've hunted everywhere!"

"No one was up, so I came out here to see the horses. The groom was combing them, so I helped," Sammy responded. When Mr. Merritt said nothing, Sammy added weakly, "I didn't know it was wrong."

"Oh, it's all right. Come along; Dolly has breakfast ready."

Breakfast sounded good to Sammy. He did not know he was the first black person to sit at the Merritt's table. He was thinking of Miss Knolls. *It is good she taught me how to eat with a fork and spoon and cut with a knife.*

Dolly blinked when she saw this unattractive young man in his strange clothes sitting in her beautifully appointed surroundings.

Sammy listened as Mr. Merritt asked Dolly to bless the food. He saw her stiff face and heard the little memorized prayer. Somehow he felt

GUESS	1. unwanted.
	2. uncomfortable.
	3. far from God.

Sammy felt uncomfortable. He listened to Mr. Merritt explain that he had to conduct a funeral this Saturday morning and was taking Sammy along.

"Not in those clothes!" Dolly gasped.

"We can stop for new clothes on the way." Mr. Merritt laughed. "I know. I know what you are thinking, Dolly. 'Man looketh on the outward appearance,' but remember, Dolly, 'the Lord looketh on the heart.' "

Sammy was glad when they were on their way in the coach.

"I must pick up two other ministers. They can take you to the clothing shop while I run another errand. Then I'll return for you, and we will still be in time for the funeral."

When the two ministers discovered Sammy in the carriage, Sammy

GUESS	1. saw their questioning looks.
	2. noticed their snobbery.
	3. heard the clothing instructions.

While Stephen Merritt went on his errand, the ministers had a good time picking out clothes for Sammy. "I never knew there was such a place!" Sammy exclaimed over the rows and rows of fine suits, sweaters, and shirts.

When Sammy finally stood before a mirror and saw himself, he exclaimed, "I don't know you, Prince Kaboo. I don't even know Sammy Morris." Then he looked for a long minute. "But God has given me

GUESS	1. a new faith."
	2. a new name."
	3. a new way to look."

Sammy thanked God for everything.

When Mr. Merritt returned, Sammy saw the approval in his eyes. He picked up the many boxes of clothing and walked to the counter to pay the bill. Even he was surprised at the sum. He told the clerk, "Where two or more Methodist preachers are gathered together, they cannot be outdone in generosity when someone else is footing the bill."

The ministers laughed. "You said, 'Nothing is too good for the boy,' remember. Now he looks like Fifth Avenue. Notice those patent leather slippers. They are the latest fashion."

Sammy saved his old clothes, however. He knew the sailors had given them in love.

Back in the coach, Mr. Merritt pointed to items of interest.

GUESS	1. "This is called Central Park."
	2. "See the Grand Opera House."
	3. "Look at that magnificent bridge."

Mr. Merritt explained the sights of New York.

Finally, Sammy said, "Did you ever pray while riding in your coach?"

"Oh, yes, I often think on spiritual things," Merritt replied.

Sammy said, "Then we will pray." He knelt down in the coach and pulled Stephen Merritt to his knees also. The two ministers remained seated but bowed their heads.

Sammy began, "Father, I have been months coming to see Stephen Merritt, so that I could talk to him about the Holy Spirit. Now that I am here, he shows me the harbor, the churches, the banks, and other things, but does not say one word about You. Fill him with Thyself, so that he will not think, or talk, or write, or preach about anything but Thee."

The burning presence of the Holy Spirit filled the soul of Stephen Merritt. He prayed as he had never prayed before. The other ministers poured out their hearts, also.

When the carriage stopped, the ministers and Sammy entered the church in a spirit of joy and glory. When Merritt preached, it seemed the heavens opened. Old things passed away. His message of comfort seemed to come from God Himself.

The remarks of the other ministers also were filled with power and inspiration. The people listened in rapture.

Sammy felt the beauty of this solemn Christian ceremony in contrast to

| GUESS |
1. the rites of the Leopard Worshipers.
2. the way dead slaves were buried.
3. the sailors, who were dropped overboard.

How different was this Christian funeral from all of that! Sammy was filled with joy because the man's soul was now

| GUESS |
1. with Jesus.
2. in heaven.
3. in the dark.

Sammy rejoiced that the Christian was now in heaven with Jesus.

The two ministers stayed at the church to talk further with those who asked how to become Christians.

Later, Merritt took Sammy in the coach to his office. There he answered Sammy's questions about the Holy Spirit. Sometimes

| GUESS |
1. Sammy seemed to be the teacher.
2. Mr. Merritt searched for answers.
3. together they searched the Scriptures.

Between them, they searched out the answers in the Bible. As they studied, both felt renewed in knowledge and spirit.

Stephen Merritt dictated a letter to the president of Taylor University, a school then in Fort Wayne, Indiana. In the letter, he said, "I'm sending you a diamond in the rough. Please polish him and send him out to enlighten the world. Let me know if you don't have room."

On the way home from the office, Mr. Merritt said, "Tomorrow is Sunday, and I'd like you to go with me to Sunday school. Would it be all right if I asked you to speak?"

"What should I say?" questioned Sammy.

"Just give your testimony and follow the leading of the Holy Spirit."

"All right," Sammy agreed. "I've never been to a Sunday school, but I'll speak if the Lord wants me to."

The Sunday school assembly was overflowing with young people. They were

GUESS	1. laughing.
	2. telling jokes.
	3. all white.

When Stephen Merritt told them a young man had come all the way from Africa to New York to learn about the Holy Spirit, the young people laughed. It seemed such a funny thing to do.

Then Sammy stood before them. He waited until all laughter stopped. "I was born a prince," he began his testimony. Slowly, quietly, he told his story. The bell rang for classes, but no one moved. Mr. Merritt had been called away for a few minutes. Sammy prayed. One by one the young people surrounded Sammy, kneeling and asking God to accept them.

When Stephen Merritt returned, he found

GUESS	1. the young people at the altar.
	2. the young people weeping.
	3. Sammy praying.

Stephen Merritt said, "Clearly the Holy Spirit has filled the entire place with His glory!"

The young people finally went to their classes where they spontaneously formed a *Samuel Morris Missionary Society*. They determined to get

GUESS	1. money for his train fare.
	2. clothing.
	3. books.

In the end they filled three trunks with things he needed for school. Dolly Merritt was one of the Sunday school teachers. No one was more eager than she to help Sammy.

At Sunday dinner, she asked Sammy to give thanks. Overcome by the kindness of everyone, Sammy expressed gratitude to his heavenly Father. After dinner Mrs. Merritt put her arm around the black boy. "Sammy, make this your home. Whatever we have we will share with you."

By the middle of the week, however, Sammy was ready for his trip to Fort Wayne, Indiana. After loving good-byes, he was alone on the train,

> | GUESS | 1. looking out the window.
> 2. overwhelmed by the great cities.
> 3. afraid of college.

Sammy wasn't afraid of college. He had no idea what it could be like. As he looked out the window of the speeding train, he was impressed with the mountains, the many cities, the roads, and the carriages. *It is so different from Africa!*

Thaddeus C. Reade, the president of Taylor University, met him at the station that Friday night.

"Welcome, Samuel Morris. Welcome to Taylor University and Fort Wayne!" He smiled and held out his hand.

Sammy took his hand gladly. His eyes sparkled. "I see why everyone wears so many clothes here. It's cold!"

"This is nothing, Sammy. Just wait until winter gets here. You *will* see cold then." President Reade liked the young man, but he kept wondering what to do with him. Obviously he wasn't ready for college work. Together they found Sammy's three trunks, and two students placed them on a wagon. When the loading was done, Sammy and the president took the coach to the school.

On the way, the president asked Sammy about the kind of room he wanted.

"If there is a room nobody wants, give that to me," Sammy said.

Later Dr. Reade wrote, "I turned away, for my eyes were full of tears. I was asking myself whether I would be willing to take what nobody else wanted. The Holy Spirit was at work in my heart the minute I met Sammy."

10

The Revival

Sammy had a sinking feeling when he woke next morning in a bare dormitory room. "I have books I can't read and more clothes than I can ever wear. I'm just a poor, ugly, black boy in an all-white college." Sammy leaped out of bed and flung himself on his knees.

"Father, oh, Father, why do You want me here? I do want to serve You among my people, but Africa seems so far away. Please help me to lean on the Holy Spirit this day!"

A bell rang, and Sammy could hear running feet and shouting. When he answered a knock on his door, he saw

GUESS

1. a red-haired young man.

2. an old man.

3. a black janitor.

A young man with freckles and the brightest red hair Sammy had ever seen spoke. "I'm Eddie from next door. Dr. Reade asked me to help you get started."

Sammy grinned. "I guess I need help. Thanks, Eddie."

"Be ready in ten minutes. Breakfast is at eight o'clock."

"Ten minutes? What's ten minutes?"

"I don't think they like me."

Eddie looked at him. "Oh, boy, you do need help! They say, 'A friend in need is a friend indeed.' Do you have a clock?"

"I have trunks of stuff—somewhere."

"They are outside your door. If you give me a hand, we will unpack after breakfast," Eddie stated. "But now, Sammy Morris, you wash up and put on your clothes—fast—that will take ten minutes."

Sammy knew what "fast" meant. He was ready before Eddie came back.

The dining hall at Taylor University was larger than any dining room Sammy could imagine. He expected to eat breakfast without being noticed, but

GUESS

1. the students stared.
2. the girls snickered.
3. some were angry.

"I don't think they like me," Sammy said.

"They don't know you. They stare at any new student who enrolls after school starts," Eddie objected.

After breakfast he and Sammy transformed Sammy's room. Now Sammy knew why he needed all three trunks. They

GUESS

1. hung curtains.
2. put down throw rugs.
3. arranged bedding.

Besides that, they hung up all of Sammy's clothes in the closet and arranged his books on the desk. Eddie showed him how to start and turn off the gas lights. "Be sure you light them every time you turn on the gas. Gas is poison unless it's burning."

What's poison? Sammy thought. He knew English, but he kept hearing new words. Eddie tried to use small words but still was surprised at what Sammy didn't know.

That afternoon President Reade was also impressed that Sammy could not fill out the application form. "I'll just enroll you as a special student," he said kindly. "Eddie, take Sammy to the ball game this afternoon and to church tomorrow. Monday morning, take him to registration, and I'll handle things from there."

Unknown to Sammy, Dr. Reade called in several professors and officers for a meeting. "We have a problem.

GUESS	1. Sammy can't read well.
	2. Sammy can't write well.
	3. Sammy can't do college work.

Since he can't read or write or understand enough for college, what shall we do?" the president appealed to his staff.

One professor answered, "It's simple; send him away. The French say, 'There's no way to change a buzzard into a hawk.' "

"Not so fast! I know Stephen Merritt, and he would not have sent the lad if he had no potential," Dr. Parker offered.

The treasurer intervened, "This is not a charity school. You know we have to skimp on meals for lack of funds. Why are we adding to our burden? I say that if the lad cannot pay his way like the other students, we don't need him."

"Dr. Parker," the president said, "I'm going to appoint you to interview Sammy and set up a course of study for him. Perhaps some of the students will give free tutoring services."

"What of his money?" the treasurer spoke bitterly.

"I personally will be responsible," said Dr. Reade. "I'm speaking at a church next Sunday and will make an appeal."

"Then I'll send the bills to you, Mr. President!"

The meeting ended on a sour note. Only Professor Parker seemed to be happy with the challenge given to him.

Dr. Reade made a strong appeal at a church in Churubusco. He told of the poor black boy who needed education to help his own tribe. He shook hands at the door, and

GUESS	1. many people gave large amounts.
	2. some gave generously.
	3. Mr. Thomas gave fifty cents.

Mr. Thomas was the only person who gave that morning.

As Dr. Reade boarded the train the next day, a butcher named

Josiah Kichler called to him, "Doctor, I heard your appeal for that poor colored boy. The Holy Spirit tells me to give this to your Faith Fund." He thrust five dollars into Dr. Reade's hand.

Later Dr. Reade told the treasurer, "This five dollars and fifty cents is the first in the *Samuel Morris Faith Fund.* It is a memorial to Josiah Kichler."

Sammy Morris objected. "The fund should not be for me. That is God's money. I want you to use it for others more worthy than I."

The Samuel Morris fund was used

GUESS	1. for Sammy's necessities.
	2. for luxuries.
	3. for other students.

Although Dr. Reade paid for necessities, Sammy never put a penny in his own pocket. Hundreds of other students also received help.*

Eddie and Sammy were becoming close friends. Eddie showed Sammy how to use the alarm clock and how to read time.

"Why is everything by time?" Sammy questioned.

"Well, they serve meals at eight A.M., twelve P.M., and six P.M. If you think time doesn't matter, you will starve." Eddie laughed. "Classes also meet at certain times." But Sammy lost interest in time.

"Eddie," Sammy said, "is there no place where black people have church? I saw in New York that they were not in the same church where I was."

"The black people here have a nice church about ten blocks from the college," Eddie responded.

"Blocks? What are blocks?"

Eddie was getting used to Sammy's questions, but he couldn't remember explaining a "block" to him. Nevertheless, he tried. "You know the streets your carriage followed to get here from the railroad station?"

"Oh, yes, the path; we have paths in Africa, too."

"Well, the ground between the paths is called a block. So you

*In the first ten years, more than two hundred students were helped.

go down ten blocks on East Wayne Street, and you are at the church."

"You mean you cross ten paths?"

"Yes, but let me take you to East Wayne Street, so you will know where to start counting."

The friends walked past the college entrance, and Eddie pointed out the sign "East Wayne."

"I can find it now, I think," Sammy said, "but it doesn't look *down* to me. It looks straight ahead."

Eddie was surprised. "I guess I did say *down* the street. Just forget it." Eddie didn't know why he said "down."

On the way back Eddie pointed out the buildings and explained their names. Sammy wondered if he would ever understand this strange world.

Back in his room, Sammy said, "Help me light the gas. This room is beautiful. It's as nice as the bishop's."

"You slept in the bishop's room? I thought his room was kept for him alone."

"I don't know," Sammy said. "That's where the Holy Spirit took me. I keep wondering what the Holy Spirit will do next!"

Eddie gave Sammy a strange look. "I'm a Christian, too, but I never think about the Holy Spirit."

"You should!" Sammy followed Eddie to the door. They said good night, and Eddie went to his room wondering why he had never talked to his heavenly Father the way Sammy did.

In spite of Eddie's explanation about the new clock, Sammy was late for church. He didn't know it could take so many minutes to walk ten blocks.

All the singing and prayers were over when Sammy walked into the beautiful church. Every seat was covered with a starched white doily, as were the arms of each seat. The members of the choir were in black robes and had just been seated. Everything was in splendid order.

The minister rose and announced his text as Sammy walked down the aisle. Sammy

GUESS	1. mounted the platform.
	2. sat in the choir.
	3. sat in the audience.

Sammy mounted the platform and confronted the minister. He said, "I am Samuel Morris. I just came from Africa, and I have

GUESS

1. a fine room at Taylor University."
2. a message for your people."
3. a new friend, Eddie."

Sammy said, "I have a message for your people."
The minister asked,

GUESS

1. "Have you been ordained?"
2. "Who sent you?"
3. "Do you have a sermon prepared?"

Sammy looked the minister in the eye. His face shone with a strange light as he said, "No sermon, but I have a message!"

The minister sat down with a puzzled expression. What Sammy said that morning was not remembered. What was remembered was the praying. While Sammy talked to his Father, as he always did, the minister and congregation were seized with

GUESS

1. a coughing spell.
2. a desire to pray.
3. a power from on high.

All fell to their knees and prayed. Some even wept. The minister said afterward, "I do not remember what was said, but I know my soul was on fire as never before. The power that brought Samuel Morris out of bondage in Africa was shining in our hearts in Fort Wayne."

When the people finally left for their homes, they realized Sammy Morris had spoken the language of the human soul. He had appealed to their heavenly Father in absolute faith.

To everyone's surprise the newspapers

1. wrote of his prayers.

GUESS	2. called the service a revival.
	3. praised the Church.

All Fort Wayne knew about the new African student who started a revival before he had been at the university a week.

11

Friends

At chapel Monday morning, Dr. Reade told the students about Sammy. He even asked for volunteers to teach the newcomer. "If you wish to help in the education of this angel in ebony, see Dr. Parker after lunch," he said.

Sammy did not hear this, for he was in

GUESS
1. administration.
2. registration.
3. recreation.

Eddie had left Sammy in the registration department as instructed. Sammy sat on a bench in the hall. He looked at

GUESS
1. the walnut paneling.
2. the colored glass above the doors.
3. the polished brass gas fixtures.

Sammy examined everything in sight. He was especially interested in the brass knocker on the door of the registrar's office. He stepped up to it and found he could lift it. When he let go, it made a great clatter, and the door opened.

A prim lady appeared. "And what is your business?" she asked.

"Dr. Reade said to come, so I'm here," Sammy stuttered.

"You must be mistaken. We have no blacks here!"

When she shut the door, Sammy went back to the bench. Soon he bowed his head in prayer. He decided he didn't like the brass knockers.

Later Dr. Reade apologized for being so late. "And now I must leave you again while I talk to the registrar for a minute."

Sammy didn't know much about time, but it seemed much longer than a minute to him before the president came back.

Dr. Reade returned with Professor Parker, who took Sammy to a small room. Sammy tried reading from several books. He finally found one that was easy for him. "Good! Good!" Dr. Parker seemed pleased. "We will begin here."

They even found a writing and spelling book like the one Mrs. Davis had used on the plantation.

"Ho, I know where I left off in this book," Sammy pointed to a page.

"Good, good!" again Dr. Parker agreed.

When he showed Sammy the arithmetic books, it was, however, another story. It seemed neither Mrs. Davis nor the missionaries had taken him past addition and subtraction. "That's all right; we have an excellent math teacher," Dr. Parker assured Sammy.

Finally, they spoke of the Bible, and Sammy's face lit up. Now he was on firm ground.

By the end of the day, Sammy knew his schedule. His classes were in

GUESS	1. reading.
	2. writing.
	3. arithmetic.

Besides those, Sammy took spelling. The only class he attended with the university students was Bible. He didn't take notes or tests but enjoyed the word of God.

Once he met his teachers and memorized his schedule, Sammy felt better. Here was work he could do and pleasant people to help him. Miss Harriet Stemen was his overall teacher and friend. Dr. Reade's daughter, Grace Husted, and a member of the faculty, Dr. Idora Rose, volunteered to aid Miss Stemen. The one who bene-fitted most from this arrangement was

GUESS	1. Miss Stemen.
	2. Sammy.
	3. Dr. Rose.

As the pupil, Sammy learned most, but Miss Stemen said, "Every day brings new blessings to me."

"Oh, Sammy," Harriet Stemen exclaimed one day in the little library room, "you are driving yourself to exhaustion studying so hard!"

Sammy looked up from his arithmetic. "I know it is hard, but 'nothing falls into the mouth of a sleeping fox.' I must try to catch up. I looked at some of Eddie's books and saw how far ahead of me he is." Sammy felt

GUESS	1. desperate to catch up.
	2. inferior.
	3. sad.

Sammy wasn't sad; he was just desperate to catch up with the other students. But it was lonely working in the little room off the library.

He was not alone for long, however. One day Harriet brought a dark Armenian boy with her. "Sammy, this is Aman. He will be studying with us."

Sammy jumped up from the desk and held out his hand. "Are you a Christian?" he asked.

"Ah, yes, I am a believer. My mother is a Bible woman in Turkey. She prays for me to be a holy man of God." Aman smiled as he put his hand in his pocket.

"And you? Do you also pray?" Sammy asked.

83

"Ah, yes. My voice rises like a fountain night and day."

"Then let us pray," Sammy proposed. The three knelt as each talked to the Father. Aman prayed, "Let this prayer of devotion, deep in my soul, rise silent to Thee."

Sammy blinked. He wondered,

GUESS	1. *Can God understand?*
	2. *Will we be friends?*
	3. *Is that praying?*

Sammy wondered if they could be friends. By the end of a week, however, Aman said, "Now my love is thawed."

Sammy took Aman's hand and laughed. "Friend, my love was never frozen. I may not always understand you, but I like you."

Aman answered, "Misunderstandings between friends only make the friendship stronger."

They learned to care for each other even when they seemed worlds apart.

Now Sammy showed Aman around the campus, explaining things. Together they attended prayer meetings.

Aman, also, had trouble with the clock and time. Sammy explained this to him, just as Eddie had done for Sammy. When he finished, Aman said, "I see the finger of the clock runs a circuit, but is still at home."

"Yes, but while it runs, it runs you—to meals, to class, to chapel, to prayer meeting. Do you understand?" Aman found it easier to wait for Sammy to take him places.

Having Aman as his friend made Sammy think of

GUESS	1. Nathan.
	2. Henry O'Neil.
	3. Margol.

Sammy thought of Henry O'Neil. He prayed for Henry so much that Aman also prayed. "Why do you pray for this one to come to America?" he asked.

Sammy answered,

GUESS

1. "Henry loves God."
2. "Henry learns fast."
3. "Henry wants to be a missionary."

Sammy said, "Henry wants to be a missionary and is smarter than I."

"What will you do about it?" Aman asked.

That question haunted Sammy. He could not

GUESS

1. pray.
2. study.
3. sleep.

Sammy had trouble sleeping, he was so concerned. Finally, he went to Dr. Reade's office. "May I speak with you, sir?"

"Why, yes, Sammy, do come in." Dr. Reade considered Sammy one of his best friends. "How can I help you?" he asked.

"I want to stop school and go to work," Sammy said.

"I'm surprised. I thought you liked it here."

"I do like it, sir, very much, but I want to earn money to bring Henry O'Neil to America."

"Oh, the young man you led to the Lord in Monrovia. I remember your telling me about him and his testimony." Dr. Reade remembered all his conversations with Sammy.

"Yes, he is more deserving than I am. He learns faster. He should have an opportunity."

"And what of your opportunity? Will you let it flutter away like a feather on the wind?"

"I don't want to, sir. I just wish Henry O'Neil could have such a chance as I have."

"Tell you what!" Dr. Reade decided. "Let me

GUESS

1. write some letters."
2. pray over it."
3. talk to friends."

85

Sammy left the office, knowing Dr. Reade would write his letters.

He was back next morning all smiles. He said,

| GUESS |

1. "Henry O'Neil is coming soon!"
2. "My Father just told me."
3. "Don't bother to write."

Sammy told the president that his Father had just told him Henry O'Neil was coming to America.

When President Reade wrote to Stephen Merritt in New York, he found out that Miss Knolls was arranging for Henry O'Neil's education in St. Louis. Sammy's prayers were answered.

12

Prayer

Dr. Reade wrote about Samuel Morris in several church papers. Because of this

GUESS
1. money was sent to the Faith Fund.
2. visitors came to see Sammy.
3. the Holy Spirit blessed the school.

Many visitors came to see Sammy. Since he never engaged in idle conversation, he worked out a plan for his visitors.

GUESS
1. He introduced himself.
2. He asked visitors to read the Bible.
3. He prayed.

The plan included these three things. Some people were startled when Sammy said, "I am reading through the Bible but find the words difficult. May I ask you to read where the last person left off?" Sammy always handed the Bible to visitors and settled down to listen.

Most visitors were happy to read and carefully checked where they left off. The students at the university found out about this and stopped into Sammy's room for reading and prayer. Soon Sammy had many student friends.

One day he was shocked because

GUESS	1. an atheist came.
	2. a preacher came.
	3. a leper came.

Even the most savage native in Kru land believed in some kind of God. Sammy had never met anyone who said, "There is no God," and called himself an atheist.

But there was an atheist on campus who heard all about Sammy. He was not satisfied with what was said in favor of Samuel Morris.

"Oh, I can put that unlearned black to shame," he boasted. "I know every argument and the answer to every Scripture." He asked a friend of Sammy's to take him to Sammy and witness his downfall. Sammy's friend laughed. "Remember Proverbs twenty-five fourteen, 'Whoso boasteth himself of a false gift is like clouds and wind without rain.' "

Sammy never admitted anyone to his room when he was praying, but after a lengthy wait, Sammy opened his door to his friend and the atheist.

After the introductions, Sammy said, "Please read the Bible where the last person checked." He handed the Bible to the atheist. The atheist threw the Bible on the table and said, "I do not read that book anymore. It is full of love affairs, wars, and a lot of big fish stories. I don't believe a word of it."

Sammy

GUESS	1. sat still.
	2. eyed the atheist.
	3. defended the Bible.

Sammy sat still and let the atheist talk. Then he rose to his feet and said, "My dear brother, your Father speaks to you, and you do not believe Him? Your Brother speaks, and you do not believe Him? The sun shines, and you do not believe it?"

Sammy paused, then continued,

GUESS	1. "God wishes to be your Father." 2. "Christ your Brother." 3. "The Holy Spirit your sun."

Sammy said all the above. Putting his hand on the atheist's shoulder, he insisted, "Kneel down, and I will pray for you."

The atheist sank down as though his life had crumbled within. But he resisted Sammy's prayers and would not open his mouth.

When the prayer was over, he stumbled to the door. Suddenly he felt a stab of pain in his heart, and he fled to his room.

Sammy, Aman, and many friends prayed for the atheist daily. A day came near the end of the semester when the atheist returned to Sammy's room.

Sammy smiled and put his hands on both shoulders of the young man.

"You are a Christian? That's what you have come to tell me?" Sammy asked.

"Yes," the atheist agreed. "I have not been able to eat or sleep or study properly. All I could think of was Jesus dying on the cross for me. My Brother, who loved me *that* much."

Together they knelt, and the one-time scoffer prayed from his heart to his Father in heaven.

Once the students on campus heard the story, many came to see Sammy.

GUESS	1. Some wanted to accept Christ. 2. Some wanted to discuss evolution. 3. Some wanted to dedicate their lives.

"Some of this so-called science takes away my faith and gives me nothing in its place," one said.

"I've been a Christian since I was a child, but all I ever thought about was getting things—power, position. I'm afraid I've been very materialistic," another exclaimed.

Even the red-haired Eddie prayed, "Oh, Father, I didn't know You were so real I could talk to You like this. I'll trust in You forever."

Sammy's room became a haven for those wishing to walk in the spirit of God.

As Sammy's reading improved, he found a biography of John Wesley and read it.

Then Sammy stopped reading and

```
┌─────────────┐
│             │   1. prayed.
│   GUESS     │   2. called to the Holy Spirit.
│             │   3. shouted.
└─────────────┘
```

Sammy prayed for all the students and for Taylor University. He did not know it, but Taylor University

```
┌─────────────┐
│             │   1. was in spiritual trouble.
│   GUESS     │   2. was in financial trouble.
│             │   3. was in physical trouble.
└─────────────┘
```

The university was at a point where it was forced to move. Colonel D. N. Foster said, "But what can we do now? Where can we go? We must move from here soon."

Lindley J. Baldwin spoke up, "Come to Upland, Indiana. We will receive you with open arms."

"I believe the Samuel Morris Faith Fund will bring in enough money to tide us over during the move," the treasurer said.

"But we would need ten thousand dollars and ten acres of land. I'm going to Sammy's room to pray," said Mr. Baldwin.

He appeared at Sammy's door very early the next morning. "I have come to pray with you," he said. "Our school is in trouble and in need of our prayers."

Together they knelt and prayed for the much needed ten thousand dollars and ten acres of land. It was an inspiring session with just

1. Sammy.
2. Lindley Baldwin.
3. the Holy Spirit.

Together Sammy and Lindley pleaded with God through the Holy Spirit. When they finished, both believed the prayer would be answered. Mr. Baldwin quoted Tennyson, "More things are wrought by prayer than this world dreams of."

Sammy held Mr. Baldwin's overcoat as he prepared to leave.

He laughed. "Sammy, you are the Moses that will lead Taylor University into the land of promise!"

Sammy

1. smiled.
2. fought to hide his tears.
3. gripped the preacher's hand.

Sammy fought back his tears. "I don't feel like a Moses," he said.

By two o'clock that same day, the ten thousand dollars had been raised along with the ten acres.

After the move to Upland was assured, a dedication service was planned. On the platform would be

1. Dr. Reade.
2. Lindley Baldwin.
3. Samuel Morris.

All the dignitaries were to attend, but it was Samuel Morris who was to give the dedication prayer and preach the sermon.

13

Competition

While everyone waited for the university to move to Upland, school in Fort Wayne continued as usual. Lessons in the little library room sometimes grew dull.

To put spark into their spelling class, Miss Stemen decided to have a spelling match between Sammy and Aman.

"It will give me a chance to shine lovely as light!" Aman smiled quietly.

"What do you mean?" After six months with Aman, Sammy still had trouble understanding him.

"You do shine with the college as a diamond. This will give me a chance to outshine you!"

"Oh, do you think you will win?" Sammy challenged.

"Ah, yes. I will receive the prize and cause your stubborn knees to bow."

"Stubborn knees! Come, come, Aman. You know my knees are the first to bow in prayer. How can you call them stubborn?"

"Now, now!" Miss Stemen said. "I didn't mean to start anything, and I said nothing of a prize."

Aman's face fell.

"All right, all right, we will have a prize," Miss Stemen amended, and she outlined the spelling contest rules.

Since it was Friday, the schoolroom was locked until Monday morning. Unfortunately,

The schoolroom looked scary in the dark.

GUESS

1. Sammy forgot his book.
2. Aman forgot his book.
3. both forgot their books.

At dinner Aman remarked, "Ah, that I had remembered my spelling book."

"Me, too," Sammy said.

"Perhaps we may lift the window in the classroom and get our books," Aman went on. "Do you agree?"

Sammy looked shocked. "You mean break into the library? Like thieves?"

"No, no, of course not like thieves—like students who forgot their books." He was startled at Sammy's objection.

"I would hate to be caught doing such a foolish thing." Sammy laughed.

The subject was dropped, but both Aman and Sammy thought about it. It occurred to Aman that he would have an advantage if he studied over the weekend. Accordingly, he

GUESS

1. set out for the library.
2. opened the window.
3. found his book.

After finding his book, he heard the sound of footsteps. Quickly, he closed the window and hid in the dark.

Sammy slipped into the library and found his book. The schoolroom looked scary in the dark, so Sammy lost no time in climbing out the window.

All weekend Sammy intended to go to Aman's room and study spelling with his friend. The student revival meetings claimed his attention, however, and he completely forgot about spelling.

Since students had been clamoring to hear Sammy's message, Dr. Reade and Miss Stemen finally agreed to let him speak at the student rally in the college auditorium.

Sammy dressed carefully. He clutched his few notes, the result of hours with Miss Stemen, and arrived at Aman's door on his way to the revival.

"You're not dressed!" Sammy objected. "You know it starts in fifteen minutes!"

"I'm not going," Aman replied. "I have to study."

Sammy nodded, hiding his surprise, and hurried to the auditorium filled with college students.

Eddie grasped his arm. "Come to the platform. Dr. Reade is waiting for you."

Looking out at the sea of faces, Sammy was

GUESS	1. anxious.
	2. proud.
	3. scared.

Sammy was scared, but he asked the Holy Spirit to lead him. Once the singing started, Sammy forgot everything but the love of God. His plain face radiated Christ's love. Clearly he had a message.

Afterward, Dr. Reade wrote, "I was so surprised at the freshness and force of Sammy's thoughts. He spoke for forty minutes in a quiet, yet earnest style, simple and natural as a child."

Everyone in the vast audience

GUESS	1. listened attentively.
	2. scorned him.
	3. profited from his words.

"All who had honest hearts to receive the truth profited from his words," Dr. Reade declared.

At the end of the meeting, crowds of students knelt with Sammy in prayer.

At breakfast on Sunday morning, everyone was discussing the revival meetings. Aman was quiet as student after student congratulated Sammy. Some said he was a "blessing to their souls," "an angel in ebony," "a messenger of God." Sammy was embarrassed at their many praises. "I wish you would give praise to Jesus, not me," he protested.

Sammy left Aman at the dining hall that Sunday, since he

96

always attended services at the Berry Street Church. A church family invited him to dinner, so he didn't get back to the campus on time to pick up his sack lunch.* Sammy usually took his sack to Aman's room. That Sunday, however, there was no answer when he knocked at the door. Sammy wondered,

GUESS
1. *Is Aman angry?*
2. *Did I say something wrong?*
3. *Where could he be?*

Sammy wondered where Aman was. Since he didn't show up, Sammy went to the revival service with Eddie.

Monday morning came too soon. Sammy was still glowing with the wonders of the revival and God's blessings as he knocked on Aman's door. "Ready for breakfast?" he said.

"Well, if the great angel in ebony hasn't come for me!" Aman acted surprised.

"I always come. What do you mean?"

"I thought God's great messenger would be too busy to bother." Aman forced a smile.

"You're joking, of course." Sammy didn't understand.

That week classes went slowly. Aman was sullen and silent as though waiting for something.

Sammy was

GUESS
1. puzzled.
2. upset.
3. befuddled.

Sammy was puzzled but studied as usual.

Friday afternoon Miss Stemen smiled. "Now is the time for the spelling contest. We shall see who wins this prize." She held up a box wrapped in flowery paper and ribbon.

The first word went to Aman. He spelled it correctly. The next word went to Sammy, who also spelled his word correctly. Then to

*Sunday nights the university students ate sack lunches to free the cooks.

Aman. "Correct." And to Sammy. "Correct." Aman spelled with confidence. It was easy to see he knew every word.

"Correct," Miss Stemen would say each time. Finally she turned to Sammy. "Either," she called out.

Sammy remembered, *I before E except after C.*

"Hum," he said. "I-E-T-H-E-R."

Aman laughed, and Miss Stemen handed him the prize. Aman unwrapped a wood carving of a monkey. He was outraged. "You call me a monkey? There is your monkey," he said, pointing at Sammy. "None of you know him; you think him good!"

"You don't? What has he done, Aman?"

"He called me a thief for suggesting we open the window to get our spelling books last Friday. Then he, himself, opens the window and studies all weekend to win the contest. He wishes to outshine me—always!"

"Sammy!" Miss Stemen said. "Did you call Aman a thief?"

"No, Miss Stemen. I said we should not open the window like thieves."

"And you should not. We lock the door, so no one should come in. But did you, Sammy?"

"Yes, Miss Stemen."

"Why?"

"I changed my mind. I decided it wasn't so bad to open the window just to get our spelling books."

"So it is true. You studied all weekend in secret to win the contest over Aman!" Miss Stemen looked disappointed.

"I was at the revival. I meant to get with Aman and study, but he wasn't in his room when I knocked; anyway, there wasn't time." Sammy felt

| GUESS |

1. that he was in trouble.
2. upset.
3. mad at Aman.

Sammy was upset. He thought that the more he defended himself, the worse he sounded.

Aman smirked. "See Miss Stemen. See how white he acts, like a lily. The students call him an angel in ebony. They don't know how he sneaks to outshine me, the son of a Bible woman."

Miss Stemen's mouth fell open. "I think we need a time of prayer."

She knelt and waited for both young men to kneel. All three were silent for a long time. Miss Stemen prayed, asking the Holy Spirit to work in the hearts of her students. Both students prayed.

Sammy stood up and clasped Aman's hands. "Dear friend, I'm sorry I offended you. Forgive me. I do not wish to outshine you or anyone. Really."

Miss Stemen touched Aman. "What have you to say? Are you sorry you were jealous?"

Aman's head dropped. "I'm very sorry I made the heavenly angels weep."

14

Fallen Leaves

Sammy arrived in Fort Wayne after the leaves had fallen, so he was totally unprepared for the array of color the next autumn. "God is surely good to you folks in Indiana," he said. "In Africa our leaves are always

GUESS

1. red."
2. green."
3. yellow."

In Liberia, West Africa, the leaves are always green. Sammy loved to

GUESS

1. walk in the woods.
2. smell wild flowers.
3. listen to songs of birds.

He had known flowers in Africa, but they lacked the scent of those in America. As he buried his nose in the flowers, he said, "This must be how heaven smells."

As they walked into the banquet room for Sammy's second Thanksgiving, Sammy told Dr. Reade about his delight with the fall colors. Above the clatter of dishes, Dr. Reade listened. He also asked questions. "Sammy, which country do you like best, Africa or America?"

Sammy answered with a question, "Which do you like best, roast turkey or raw monkey?"

"Why, Sammy, you didn't eat monkeys!"

"Oh, yes. I ate monkeys and ate them raw."

Dr. Reade decided to change the subject. "Does it bother you, being the only black person here?"

"No, sir," Sammy answered. "When I knocked off a small piece of skin and found I was white under the black, I put black ink over it. I was afraid there might be a white spot when it healed."

Dr. Reade laughed. "I'm glad we have made you feel at home here!"

"I'm glad I'm black. When I go back to preach to my own people, they will listen." It wasn't often Sammy spoke of this dream. Sometimes it seemed

GUESS	1. years away.
	2. it would never come true.
	3. he would go tomorrow.

Sammy sometimes felt his dream would never come true.

"I have a favor to ask of you, Sammy," the president said. "You have rejected the idea of a photograph before, I know, but I'm writing your story for a church paper, and I really need a picture of you. Will you agree?"

Sammy looked at his friend and said, "It is just that I am so ugly. I want people to see Jesus, not me."

Sammy

GUESS	1. agreed to the picture.
	2. refused again.
	3. said he would think about it.

Sammy finally agreed.

After the plates of turkey arrived and there was a lull in the general conversation, Dr. Reade turned to Sammy and asked, "How do you like our snow?"

Sammy laughed. "Do you know that we have no word for snow in the Nigrite language? I was so amazed when I looked out one morning and saw it, I

GUESS

1. ran outside."
2. gathered a handful."
3. melted the snow."

Sammy ran outside and gathered a handful of snow.

He went on speaking. "When the snow melted, I said, 'Where did it go? It has left only a few drops of water!' If I could understand, Dr. Reade, I think God sends us messages from heaven in the snow."

The president agreed. "We do need to thank our Maker for 'all things bright and beautiful,' as the song says."

"You know," Sammy reflected, "a year here is worth a lifetime in Africa."

Happily, he settled down to eat his Thanksgiving dinner. Such a feast it was!

"Another thing I want to talk about is the city revival," Dr. Reade began as he put his fork into the pumpkin pie.

"What revival?" Sammy loved preaching.

"This revival is for all of Fort Wayne. The only building large enough is the roller skating rink on west Main Street. The meetings will be held there, though it will be cold, I know."

"What can I do to help?" Sammy asked.

"We want you to sit on the platform and pray. Your very presence will count for God."

Sammy agreed and asked a lot of questions about

GUESS

1. prayer.
2. the Bible.
3. roller skating.

Sammy had never heard of roller skating and asked about it.

"I'd like to try it one day," Sammy decided, after hearing the description.

"Well, don't bite off more than you can chew," the president warned. "If you didn't learn as a child, you could get hurt trying it now."

Sammy laughed. "There is a saying, 'Be sure to keep an eye out for what you can swallow, and also for what can swallow you.'"

Dr. Reade laughed. "Exactly! You always amaze me, Sammy." They left the banquet laughing.

So Sammy attended the revival meetings. Every night he was on the platform. Sometimes he sang; sometimes he helped. Always he prayed.

The winter of 1892-1893 was exceptionally cold. In January Sammy caught a cold, so

GUESS

1. he stayed home.
2. he stayed in bed.
3. he attended the services.

Sammy continued to attend services even when the temperature was twenty degrees below zero and the night was dark and stormy. The ministers said,

GUESS

1. "His face inspires us!"
2. "His faith inspires us!"
3. "His coughing disturbs us!"

Sammy smothered his coughing. The ministers admired his simple faith.

At the final meeting, Sammy was asked to lead the congregation in singing the hymn "Tell Me the Old, Old Story of Jesus and His Love." No one forgot

1. the light on Sammy's face.

GUESS
2. his beautiful voice.

3. his holy manner.

Sammy seemed to have a holy light on his face as he sang. He was filled with the love of the Holy Spirit, and many awoke to Christ's call.

Though Sammy couldn't shake his cold, he continued to attend classes. His strength

GUESS
1. was better.

2. weakened.

3. failed.

Sammy's strength failed, and he finally had to admit he was gravely ill. "Why didn't you tell us sooner?" Miss Stemen admonished.

Aman went with Sammy to St. Joseph's Hospital and was impressed by everyone's concern.

Sammy said, "When I froze my ears last winter, they hurt me very much. I asked my Father about it, and they quit hurting me right away. Now, I cannot get well. I don't understand it."

After weeks of pneumonia, Sammy finally said, "I understand it now." He looked up from his hospital bed into the eyes of Dr. Reade, and said,

GUESS
1. "I have seen the angels coming."

2. "I was saved for a purpose."

3. "I have fulfilled my purpose."

Sammy said that he had fulfilled God's purpose for him. "My work here on earth has been finished."

"What about your work among the people in Africa?" Dr. Reade protested.

"It is not 'my work.' It is Christ's work. He must choose His own workers. Others can do it better."

The next day Sammy died. His hymnbook was on his lap opened to his favorite hymn.

> Fade, fade, each earthly joy.
>   Jesus is mine,
> Break every tender tie,
>   Jesus is mine!

15

Yet He Speaketh

The body of Samuel Morris lay in the college chapel until the day of the funeral. Then ten students, among them Aman and Eddie, carried the coffin the ten blocks to the Berry Street Church. The street was lined on both sides with

GUESS
1. students.
2. churchgoers.
3. faculty members.

All those bared their heads as the body of Samuel Morris was carried to the church. Many were unable to get into the church service, but they waited outside and

GUESS
1. attended the graveside ceremony.
2. prayed.
3. wept.

The graveside ceremony was the largest ever seen in Fort Wayne. Because the cemetery was divided, with white people buried on one side and blacks on the other, Sammy was buried in the space between as a strong link between the two.

His monument reads:

Samuel Morris—1873-1893
Prince Kaboo
Native of West Africa
Exponent of the Spirit Filled Life

Dr. Reade said, "Samuel Morris was a divinely sent messenger of God to Taylor University. He came to prepare himself, but his coming prepared the university for a missionary training program."

A few days after Sammy's death, the students held a prayer meeting. Eddie rose and said, "I feel impressed I must go to Africa in Sammy's place. I pray that as his work has fallen upon me, so the mantle of his faith may likewise fall upon me."

Two other students also dedicated their lives to missions that night.

In later years, multitudes of students yielded to the Holy Spirit when they heard Sammy's story. Eventually, Taylor University Bible School was established in Africa. There, native Christians were trained as teachers and evangelists.

Because Sammy lived and died a spirit-filled life

GUESS

1. black people were saved.
2. white students became missionaries.
3. natives of Africa became evangelists.

Even the lives of Stephen Merritt and Dr. Reade changed. Aman, too, dedicated his life to following the Holy Spirit. The Berry Street Church had to enlarge to accommodate new members. The Samuel Morris Faith Fund helped hundreds of students prepare for the mission field.

Sammy's story was translated into five languages. Only God knows of the Holy Spirit's influence because of his life.

Several years after Sammy's death, Stephen Merritt heard a knock on his door. "Come in," he called. "Have a seat."

An old sea captain seated himself, removed his hat, and said, "Sir, I've come to ask about Sammy Morris. What happened to him?"

Stephen Merritt smiled. "He set Taylor University on fire with the Holy Spirit."

"Like he did my ship!" The captain laughed delightedly. "Where is he now?"

"With Jesus. He never reached twenty-one years of age, but dozens of Taylor students have taken his place on the mission field."

The captain was stunned. "He offered the first prayer on my ship. My men are waiting now to find out what happened. I'm so sorry he is dead."

"He is dead, yet he speaketh." Stephen Merritt looked into the captain's eyes. Together they bowed their heads as Dr. Merritt prayed, "Oh, God, I pray the Holy Spirit will touch young people every day to believe—as Sammy Morris believed."

Moody Press, a ministry of the Moody Bible Institute, is designed for education, evangelization, and edification. If we may assist you in knowing more about Christ and the Christian life, please write us without obligation: Moody Press, c/o MLM, Chicago, Illinois 60610.